VICKI LAWRENCE & MARC ELIOT

Vicki!

THE TRUE-LIFE ADVENTURES OF MISS FIREBALL

SIMON & SCHUSTER
New York London Toronto Sydney Tokyo Singapore

SIMON & SCHUSTER
Rockefeller Center
1230 Avenue of the Americas
New York, NY 10020

SIMON & SCHUSTER and colophon are registered trademarks
of Simon & Schuster Inc.

Designed by Pei Koay
Manufactured in the United States of America

10 9 8 7 6 5 4 3 2 1

Library of Congress Cataloging-in-Publication Data
Lawrence, Vicki.
    Vicki!: the true-life adventures of Miss Fireball/Vicki Lawrence
and Marc Eliot.
        p.   cm.
    1. Lawrence, Vicki, 1949–   . 2. Television personalities—United
States—Biography.   I. Iliot, Marc.   II. Title.
PN1992.4.L35A3   1995
791.45'028'092—dc20
    [B]   94-46710
                                                            CIP

ISBN 0-684-80286-4

Lyrics to "Al" used by permission of Ken Welch and Mitzie Welch.
(credits continued on page 239)

DEDICATED TO AL—

My sweet, intense Al

My strong, immense Al

We shall overcome . . .

—From "Al," **by Ken and Mitzie** Welch

A n d   .   .   .

TO MY FANS

Cry every day
Laugh every day
Think every day
Don't give up.
Don't ever give up.

—Jim Valvano

Others may hate you.
But those who hate you don't win
unless you hate them back.
Then you destroy yourself.

—Richard Nixon

CONTENTS

Acknowledgments

Thanks to David and Sandy Brokaw for their time and thoughtfulness, and most particularly for their incessant schmoozing with Al in the audio booth where this book was conceived. Thanks also to Mel Berger, my literary agent, and Bob Asahina, my editor, for helping to make the concept a reality.

A collective thanks to Gail Ott, Jimmy Smith, and Eduardo Santiago, and everyone who helped gather facts and photos. Thanks to David Michaels for helping with so much of the tedious legwork and endless fact-checking.

Thanks to my kids, Courtney and Garrett, who remind me daily what's really important.

Special thanks to Marc Eliot, who now knows me better than he ever wanted to, and still seems to be smiling, God love him. He made what I had feared would be a dreadful, insurmountable task a surprisingly pleasurable one.

And then there's Carol . . . I often say that I feel like I went to the Harvard School of Comedy in front of America. I'm closer to Carol now than when I was a kid on her show. My respect and admiration, not only for her talent, but her work ethic, has clarified and deepened with time. When I was on *The Carol Burnett Show* my co-workers often used to tell me how lucky I was and that I wouldn't even know what "show biz" was really like until I went out into the real world. Carol's show was a haven for me.

Acknowledgments

I was a child with few responsibilities. Now that the responsibility is mine, I appreciate even more what a special privilege it was. I want to pass on to as many people as I can the camaraderie, the mutual respect for others, and the laughter that permeated Carol's set, and those eleven years of my life.

Thanks is really not word enough for Carol. Yes, she plucked me out of obscurity, but more than that she taught me to be productive, to be good to one another, and most of all—to laugh.

Introduction

During the weeks that followed the cancellation of my talk show in June 1994, my mind and body were affected by just about every conceivable emotion. I was in an impossible relationship with the president of Group W, my show's distributor, and although I had made it clear I simply could not continue to work for him under the present conditions, and that giving him an ultimatum might mean the end of my show, I nevertheless was unprepared for the axe when it finally fell.

Even though my husband, entire staff, and crew agreed that getting away from Group W would be the best thing that could happen to me, I was still shocked. In my heart I had hoped someone in that organization would realize that saving *Vicki!* was a high priority. I was wrong.

After the initial shock, I felt an overwhelming sense of guilt. My family depended upon me, as did my staff. Now, we were all unemployed. I would frequently wake up in the middle of the night—in the dark, in a sweat, my heart pounding, my stomach a huge knot. Perhaps I should have done whatever it took to make my relationship with Group W work. I would replay the events of the past two years over and over in my mind . . .

Me and what's-her-face.

I Thought Show Business Was Supposed to Be Fun!

At the final taping of the second season of *Vicki!,* my nationally syndicated talk show, I took a moment to look around at all the people on my staff who'd done such a terrific job to make this show work. I felt really proud because we'd managed to never vary from what we set out to do from the minute we launched the show. Of all the things I'd done in my professional life, it was the talk show that seemed most to fit my talent like a beautifully tailored glove. What's more, it was the most fun thing I'd ever done.

However, for all that, I knew there was a strong possibility that the taping I'd just completed might very well have been the show's last. The owners of *Vicki!*, Group W, a Westinghouse corporation, and I had never really meshed as a team. The unavoidable problem was, we had diametrically opposed views as to how the business end of "show business" should be conducted.

A few weeks later I got a call at home from my publicist, Sandy Brokaw, who'd just spoken with a reporter from *Variety*, to check on a rumor that I was being replaced. That was the first time we'd heard of any impending decisions on Group W's part. Sandy and I decided to say nothing until Westinghouse's official word. We didn't have to wait long. As of the last week in June, I was out.

The feeling I had was like being on a speeding train that's suddenly run out of track. Now, I found myself spending all my time at home, which began to feel more like a prison than a sanctuary.

Being fired also put an incredible strain on my relationship with Al, who had watched me go through the most stressful period of my life. I had never been fired from anything before, and I knew it was breaking his heart to see me go through this.

Al, of course, is Al Schultz, my husband, the only person in the world who would literally throw his body in front of a truck for me, something he had done repeatedly during the past two years—figuratively of course. You must understand, a lot of the movers and shakers in Hollywood have a real thing about the type of strong marriage we have, *as in, it totally pisses them off!* When they want to get to you, and they always seem to want to sooner or later, they don't appreciate your having someone standing solidly between you and them for protection. Agents, managers, producers, distributors all seek to manipulate you in one way or another. Unfortunately, that's as much a part of the business as makeup and applause. I believe one of the things that early on had gotten Group W angry was Al's refusal to simply get out of the way.

In truth, Group W had tried to fire me a year earlier. At one point in 1993, I stood in front of my bathroom mirror late on a June night and asked myself out loud, "Am I the only insane person in a business that is totally sane?"

"It's just possible," my reflection answered, "you're the only sane person in a perfectly insane business!" Either I had the smartest reflection in the world, or I was truly losing my mind.

One day, I decided to call Roseanne. If anyone had been through what I was going through now, and lived to talk about it, it was Roseanne.

I dialed her office number and got her assistant on the phone, a fellow named Mo. "How may I help you, Miss Lawrence."

I said to myself, oh man, they must get all kinds of screwy calls. He's not going to believe this is "Miss Lawrence" at all. I started sobbing into the phone, nearly incoherent, about all that was going on, and he said, "All right, calm down, Vicki, make yourself a drink. It's noon and Rosey's got some things going on right now, but she's free this afternoon and will call you around four."

"Okay, Mo, and thanks," I sniffled into the phone, and hung up, never for a second believing she would ever actually call me back, until promptly at four, when the phone rang. I picked it up and heard that familiar flat nasal voice on the other end.

"Hullo?"

"Roseanne?"

"Yeah."

"Do I call you Roseanne or Rosey?"

"Whatever."

"I'll call you Rosey, because I feel like I know you."

"That's cool. What's the problem?"

Once I started, I couldn't stop. I talked to her about everything that was going down and she gave me some pretty solid advice. Don't cry, buck up, that sort of thing.

19

Then she paused and added, "Group W . . . Aren't those the same sons of bitches who fucked over Mike Douglas?"

"Yep," I said, "those are the ones."

She then went into long lecture mode. "I've been watching you for years, I'm a big fan of yours and so is Tom. You're a really good comedienne, but you're even better at hosting a talk show. You have to be very specific about what you need to survive. Nail it down and then be prepared to lose it all, because that's the only way you'll get it."

What Roseanne said made a lot of sense to me. I'd been in this business a long time, and had seen firsthand all the nonsense that goes on. Working on *The Carol Burnett Show* under the iron-fist rule of her producer and husband, Joe Hamilton, was the best lesson anyone could ever get in the facts of show business life. On stage, Carol was the star, but behind the camera it was Joe who wielded all the power.

I think some people's learning arc is steeper than others'. Mine has had a nice, slow, gentle curve to it, and reached its zenith when I finally got my own talk show. Maybe that's why, after nearly thirty years in show business, I didn't feel I really needed a lot of pencil-pushing executives teaching me overnight what I had already spent a lifetime learning.

We started taping the *Vicki!* show in early July 1992, a practice "startup week" to make sure we were all on the same team and knew what we were doing. We were scheduled to premiere on the air August 31. Two weeks prior to that we were going to start taping for real, and bank a number of shows.

Looking back, those first shows were a disaster. They were overbooked, the production values were wrong, and they were built around topics I would never do. Such as "Putting the X in Sex," complete with men who'd had penile implants. Group W hated them, and so did I.

So we shut down. I knew that besides subject matter, one of the prime ingredients missing on our team was a father figure in the booth. The director we'd originally hired was something of a tyrant, on stage more than he was in the booth, screaming at people, basically I think because he was lost. I've never been able to tolerate people who do that sort of thing.

However, when I tried to have him replaced, Group W resisted. Finally, when they agreed to let him go, a number of them told me they hadn't liked him to begin with. Oh.

My executive producer, Nancy Alspaugh, and I interviewed a lot of directors in a relatively short period of time, until we found Arthur Forrest. As soon as he walked in, I knew he was the one. Quiet, calm, sensible. *A father figure!* I liked him a lot.

Two weeks later, with a new director and a zillion meetings behind us, we all felt back on track and started taping for real. Our premiere show was "My Teen Favorites," including Fabian, Frankie Avalon, and Annette Funicello. Needless to say, it was quite a different show than the Penile Implant Parade.

Still, there were some problems that persisted with some staffers. I found myself constantly complaining that we were overbooking shows, that I was spending too much time introducing people and not enough time talking to them. I kept having to remind Group W that the show was conceived to be *entertainment*-driven, and that was why it was hosted by an *entertainer.*

From the beginning, then, there was this friction, which led to a serious division of loyalties. If push came to shove, I believed, I was the only one truly indispensable. After all, the show was still called *Vicki!*

Even as our backstage struggles continued, the show, which had been an instant success, continued to do extremely well. We received excellent reviews and had terrific November sweeps ratings. This confirmed to me that my instincts had been correct, that the whole point of my show was that it wasn't like anything else on daytime TV.

My favorite shows were always the personal ones, fortified with terrific celebrity guests. Issue-oriented shows that I occasionally did were fine too, which is why Oprah, Phil, Sally, Geraldo, and a million interchangeable others do them. However, because I'm known primarily as an entertainer, I had an advantage that allowed me to bring something unique to daytime TV.

We produced what I consider to be a number of truly memorable shows. Nineteen ninety-two's Christmas Eve program comes to mind as one that will always be one of my favorites. Carol was on it, and so was Betty White. The funny thing was, we received more feedback from men off that show than women. I think one reason was because they're home Christmas Eve day, and so a lot of men who don't normally get to see us happened to see that show. It was a lot of fun, even if it did get a little raunchy. When Carol gets a bit risqué, the audience always forgives her, because she never "gets it" at first. Carol was telling a story about singing "O Come All Ye Faithful" and somehow in the context of the interview, the meaning of the title got taken the wrong way. Then Betty came out and brought it all up again, and things just got real silly.

We did a week of "Vicki's Fantasies," which were really a lot of fun. We did a different one every day. For my first, I got to interview Garth Brooks. He was so charming. What a truly delightful guy. During the interview, Al was standing backstage with Garth's manager. At one point she turned and asked, "How do you let your wife just blatantly flirt with Garth like that?"

Al said, "Well, he's a lot younger and a lot richer than I am. What am I going to do?"

Day two I got to meet Michael McDonald from the Doobie Brothers. I just wanted to sit in his lap and have him play the piano around me! The third day I had Fess Parker on. You know, Davy Crockett. I was so in love with him when I was a kid. I wanted him to be my dad. He is a vintner up in Santa Barbara now and doesn't really do much in show business these days, but when I called him he hopped right on a plane and flew to Burbank. He's still fabulous-looking! And so sweet! *Dad!*

The next week, as a payback, I decided to do a show built around "Al's Fantasies." Let me tell you, putting those together took all of five minutes. Every guy at the studio was glued to our set that day. We couldn't get rid of them!

Al's fantasies were, first, having the Laker girls come out and dance for him, then Gabrielle Reese, the pro beach volleyball player who's quite an eyeful, then a Playboy Playmate lingerie fashion show, and, finally, Bob Golic, former Raider, because Al loves football.

At the end of the show, Al proposed to me, which I didn't know he was going to do. He announced on the air he wanted to marry me all over again on our twentieth anniversary, and that he would do it anywhere in the world I wanted! Everyone kept knocking on my office door making suggestions. What about Palm Springs? *Anywhere in the world,* I kept reminding them. Somebody then suggested Hawaii! Hey, guys! *World* is the key word here! Let's get with the program!

After we finished taping, we took a photo of Al surrounded by Playboy bunnies, and as a joke I placed an ad in *Variety* that said: "For your consideration—Big Al, special guest star on the Vicki Show, this Thursday," and on the bottom, "looking for representation."

We did a *This Is Your Life* style show called "Vicki's Crushes," with some of the guys I had crushes on when I was a kid, including Jan and Dean, Jimmy Darren, and John Davidson. Lyle Waggoner played Ralph Edwards. At the end of it, as all the guys were pretending to fawn all over me, Al suddenly appeared carrying a picket-type sign with arrows pointing to his head that said "Vicki's Husband." He played it for all it was worth, and that remains one of the best laughs we ever got on the show.

When we had Hugh Hefner on, we went on location and shot the entire show at the mansion. It's a slice of Americana now, we all grew up hearing and reading about it. We shot some footage in the morning, from ten to one. In the famous grotto are little water wings now and baby stuff, like floating duckies. I looked at it and said to myself, I hope he gave the grotto a really good acid bath before he let his kids in it! We took a lunch break, and then I finally got to sit down and actually talk with Hef. I was more than a bit nervous because the entire morning people kept running up to me and saying, "He seems to be in a really good mood, things are great and he's really looking forward to this . . ."

By the time I actually met him it was like meeting the Pope. Before we actually did the show, we kept wondering what I would wear to the mansion. I finally decided on these gorgeous Donna Karan silk pajamas, since Hef always wears pajamas. I also brought along my daughter's bedroom slippers, which are moose feet with big horns on them. I hoped to break the ice by flashing him my horny feet. When Hef saw them, he went and put on the bunny slippers his daughter had given him. Well, he turned out to be the nicest guy. I really enjoyed him. I decided his problem was that before he married Kimberly he'd been hanging around with the wrong women all those years!

We did a show with Ann Jillian. I thought it would be good to have her on and talk about all that she'd been through, including breast cancer and having a baby at the age of forty-two. She'd been on the cover of every magazine, and it was obvious to me that women were fascinated by her. Her husband appeared during the show, and she sang a lullaby to her baby. It was a wonderful show, and drew great ratings, as I knew it would.

Doris Day was another neat guest. I just adored her when I was growing up. She doesn't do talk shows. Everyone has asked her, to no avail. So, imagine how excited I got when she invited me to Carmel for a big charity event for one of her animal causes. Once again we opened up the show, left the studio, and shot footage of the event, and the rest of the show the next day at her hotel in Carmel.

After, I thought it was one of my better interviews. I almost felt like Barbara Walters. She did say she really got screwed in her marriage to Marty Melcher. Just the idea of someone screwing Doris Day made me want to kill! I couldn't help but ask how she kept smiling. How did she stay "Doris Day"?

We shot some of it in a bar, and Doris asked the bartender to pour her favorite drink. I thought, God, Doris Day drinks? Maybe I should order a Shirley Temple. I asked her what she was going to have and she said her favorite was Absolut Citron. I said, "Well, pour one of those up for me! I'm drinking vodka with Doris Day!"

Mickey Rooney, God bless him, was wired the day I interviewed him. I was lucky, he's usually either wired or in a coma. He didn't remember me, even after I reminded him that we had done the Burnett show together, one of our classic sketches, "The Funn Family." He looked at me, lowered his voice and said, "I wasn't there, sweetie."

Fair enough, Mick.

As I said, I was also willing to do shows built around issues. What Al and I were learning was that as long as they didn't become too doctrinaire, themes and topics clearly worked on daytime. For instance, I did a "Teens Talk" show inspired by a column Al read in the paper one day where teenagers wrote about their problems and other teenagers answered them. For instance, "Why if girls claim to care about nothing but your brain and your manners do they always go out with the captain of the football team when prom time comes around?" We talked about sex, drugs, rock and roll, all of it. The kids we had on were very open, and it made for a really interesting show.

I also learned I could have the same people back again for shows with totally different themes. For instance, I could have Steve Allen on to talk about late-night television and I know he's going to have a lot to say. I could then have him back the following week with his wife, Jayne Meadows, to talk about long-lasting marriages in Hollywood. And I could have him back again when I did celebrity authors. I found that when I used a celebrity on a theme show I could get more from them than if I just did strictly promotional interviews, which to the viewer translates into oh, they're back again, what are they plugging this time? I considered all of it part of the process of learning how to do the best talk show possible.

And yet, in spite of what I considered a solid start, the support that I continued to receive came mostly from the guest stars on the show, and from those staffers who remained loyal to me, "The Branch DaVickians," as Jay Leno laughingly referred to them one day backstage at NBC.

I knew the show's achievement was no accident. After all, Al and I have been in television forever. As time went on, I thought I deserved a little recognition for it from Group W. After all, we had successfully returned them to daytime TV, from which they'd been absent for ages, their last hit show being *Hour Magazine*.

What I got instead was a long series of increasingly hostile encounters that led up to a climactic battle over control of the direction, content, and style of my show.

From the beginning, my title had been "co-executive producer." However, when push came to shove, Derk Zimmerman, the president of Group W Productions, told me it was only a courtesy title, that Group W never intended for me to have any real behind-the-scenes power.

Then, in January 1993, we decided to do a show built around kids who wanted to be made over to look like their favorite teen stars on *Beverly Hills 90210*. We booked José Eber, who is, in my estimation, the best in the business.

We also booked Shanice, a very talented gal, who'd just received a Grammy nomination for her hit song, "I Love Your Smile," and was supposed to sing it on the show.

On top of that we also booked a young man named David Burke who had written two books on teen street talk.

At this point I said to Nancy, "Stop, time out, the show is overbooked!" Instead, when the taping day came, I was informed that we had added yet another guest, a young rap artist named Yolanda "Yo-Yo" Whitaker. She wanted to do two of her rap songs, which were so obscene they could never be broadcast on daytime TV. She ended up sitting on the panel.

We got to where Shanice was scheduled to sing her song and Nancy decided to cut it in half. It came to a screeching halt. I was furious.

Al was upset as well. He walked out of the audio booth, where he usually sat during taping, and ran head-long into our talent gal, Joyce Coleman, standing with four men in suits. She asked Al what was wrong and he told her he was really pissed off the way Shanice was handled, and that he was going out for a breath of fresh air. At that point she said, "Al, I'd like you to meet these gentlemen from Motown."

He looked at them and said, "Are you happy with this?"

They said, "Not at all, but we were told you were out of time."

Al stuck his head in the directing booth and said, "Nancy, redo the number."

"We can't redo the number," she said. "We're out of time."

"Redo the entire number!"

•   •   •

*F*rom that point on, there was very little spontaneous communication between my staff and me concerning the theme and content of shows. According to Group W, from this point on, any meetings I wished to have with my staff had to be scheduled in advance and approved by Group W. At one point I called Geraldo Rivera, in New York, because I'd heard he'd had similar problems.

"My advice to you, Vicki," he said, "is to hang in until the end of your first season. That's the time to get things straightened out. Group W will have all their stations lined up for the coming year and you'll have your best leverage."

About this time, early January, I began seeing a doctor about a pain I had developed in my stomach that wouldn't go away. I was sure it was connected to the growing stress I felt over the continuing tug-of-war between Group W and me. I called my pediatrician first and asked what he thought I should do. He said he'd prescribe some Valium for me.

"No," I said, "you don't understand."

"Okay," he said, "Halcion."

"*You don't understand!*" I finally convinced him I thought there was something physically wrong, and he sent me to Dr. Lyons, a respected internist in Long Beach, where I live. As he examined me I began talking about what was going on behind the scenes at *Vicki!*

"You have all the classic symptoms of someone suffering from too much stress. Gee, I thought show business was fun," he said to me.

"It's supposed to be."

My staff, at least the Branch DaVickians, couldn't help feeling caught in the middle. At this point, a number of them simply threw up their hands and quit, unable to take it anymore. That really upset me, and I decided I had to do something. I couldn't wait until the end of the season. But what?

I decided to call Bill Korn, Derk Zimmerman's boss, whose office was in New York. I told him about the problem I was having, and he assured me we would get together and work everything out the next time he came out to Los Angeles.

So we got together, and after our meeting, in which I expressed the need for more control over my show, and which it appeared I might actually get, I hoped the last six weeks of the season would pass without any further incidents.

And, for a while, everyone's morale did pick up and things seemed to go smoother. The last week in March, the staff and I went to a little Mexican restaurant across the street from the studio to celebrate my birthday. Even Derk came by. At one point he took me aside and told me his birthday gift to me was the good news that Group W was picking up my option for year two. I put down my margarita and started laughing. Derk asked what was so funny.

I said, "Well, I guess I figured that when you picked up the show's option in February you had picked up mine as well. After all, Derk, how could you do the Vicki show without Vicki?" This happened at the same time I was nominated for my first Emmy as Outstanding Talk Show Host.

Not a word of congratulations came from him. Instead, one morning, about three weeks from the end of the season, Derk called Al and said, "I just want you to know I'm sending in a new guy on Monday, Donn Fletcher, to kind of keep tabs on the last of this season's shows."

Al asked him what he meant by keeping tabs.

"Oh, just to be my eyes and ears."

When Al got off the phone and told me what Derk said, I asked the same question. What did Derk mean by keeping tabs? Neither of us had any idea.

Sure enough, when I walked in Monday morning, Fletcher was there. I walked up and what can I say, I lost it. I'm embarrassed to tell you that in front of everybody I called him a dickhead to his face. He just stood there calmly and said, "Vicki, now, I'm here to be your friend, and if you'll just calm down . . ."

Calm down? I went ballistic! "Why are you here?" He gave me the same answer I'd gotten from Derk—the "eyes and ears" routine. At this point I went into my office and called my personal attorney, Gregg MacGregor, and told him I was walking off the show. He advised me to come over to his office immediately. He thought we all needed to meet before anything else happened.

When I arrived at Gregg's, he said he thought it best that everyone convene at his office to try to resolve the situation. I explained once more that I had no idea why this new fellow was there, unless maybe it was to spy on Al and me.

A short time later, Derk showed up at Gregg's office, with good old "eyes and ears" and Group W's in-house attorney. Derk began the meeting reading from a prepared statement, after which I asked him flat out if it was more important for Donn Fletcher to be on the set than me, and he said yes. "There are only three weeks left to the season. Whatever problems we have, can't we iron them out during hiatus?"

He said no.

At that point I felt the pain return to my stomach, worse than ever. The next day I went to see Dr. Lyons, who said I was under too much stress and ordered me to take two weeks off and get some real peace and quiet.

That's when things really went bonkers. Group W insisted on finishing the season with guest hosts. The next day Alley Mills, Christina Ferrare, and Shari Belafonte-Harper's names were bandied around in the trades as possible replacement hosts. In one article, *Variety* quoted

Group W as saying, "If we can find a [permanent] replacement for Vicki in the next two weeks, we will do it."

My personal assistant, Gail, was given her two-weeks' notice by Group W and ordered to clear everything out of my office and send it to my house. One of my staff members arrived at the house and dumped the contents of my entire office in my garage. I took one look at all the boxes and cried.

I stayed away for the next three weeks, until the official end of the season, during which time Group W made good on their threat and used guest hosts in my place. There were eighteen shows left when I got sick, and I think they managed to do about twelve. At one point someone in the press asked me, "Do you honestly think that you have two friends who will back you up in this town? Don't you think that other celebrities are so selfish and so single-minded that when push comes to shove they won't care about you or your career?"

As it turned out, people did care. I received a lot of support from my peers. Every major celebrity who'd been scheduled to be on as a guest for the remainder of the season canceled. I found that kind of encouragement and support overwhelming.

A day or so later, my publicist, Sandy Brokaw, called to say I needed to think about talking to the *National Enquirer.* At first I refused.

"Well," Sandy said, "they've gotten their hands on some stuff. It's Friday," he said. "Sleep on it. By Monday you might want to talk to them. Sometimes you can get them to listen."

Monday afternoon, while I was taking my son, Garrett, to a doctor's appointment, I got a call from Al on the car phone saying that I needed to call the *Enquirer* immediately.

"Why?"

"It's really ugly, Vicki. I just talked to Sandy and he has

a copy of what they're going to run, unless you speak to them."

Now Al and I have always laughed about the fact that most of the time we can't get *into* the *Enquirer* because we're so boring. I thought for a second, hey, maybe I should be flattered by all of this!

So, while Garrett was in the doctor's office, I sat in my car for an hour and talked to a reporter from the *Enquirer* by the name of Tony Frost. Tony began by telling me he had "stuff" about Al sexually harassing women on the show's staff!

I said, "That's pretty strong, Tony."

"Well, let me find the exact quote, Miss Lawrence. Here it is, 'Al said to one of the women one day, My, that skirt certainly shows off your goods.' "

I started laughing. "That sounds like a line out of a bad movie. That skirt shows off your *goods?* Oh yeah, that's something Al would say."

Tony also claimed I had turned the show into a war zone, that they had documentation that Al and I both drank too much, and that I ran around calling Carol Burnett "the C word."

"Let me tell you something, Tony," I said. "I owe Carol Burnett every nice thing that's ever happened to me in my life, and to tell you the truth I can't believe I'm defending myself to you people."

I hung up, called Al and said I felt I had just wasted my time trying to reason with the magazine. They didn't want to hear that I loved Carol, they didn't want to hear anything that implied I loved my work, and anyway, I had no more time to talk because Garrett's doctor was waiting for his check.

Before the article actually ran, Sandy was able to get an advance copy. It turned out because I had actually talked to Tony, he had tried to get some of the more "colorful" things taken out. Still, they had Al pumped up to 275 pounds, a "huge gorilla of a person" and there was a lot of the usual "insiders said" nonsense, balanced with a few of my direct quotes.

While all this was going on, my attorney, Gregg, and Group W's attorneys got together and worked through the summer to arrive at a resolution of sorts. Sometime in August, a formal agreement was drawn up and sent off to Bill Korn in New York.

I had insisted that either Al was hired on as an official consultant, or I was out of there. Gregg had been sure that was going to be the deal-breaker, but I told him I no longer cared. I was prepared to lose it all. I had finally arrived precisely at that place where Roseanne had said I would. And that, of course, was when Group W gave in, signed the agreement, hired Al, and acknowledged me as a full executive producer, in fact as well as name.

We went back into production that fall, and premiered our second season with a lineup of 192 affiliates. With all the growing pains behind us, I looked forward to what I hoped would be smooth sailing from there on in. Little did I know it would prove to be anything but . . .

One of the most interesting things that happened that summer occurred when Char, the psychic, was asked, in my absence, to be a guest host. She called me one evening to tell me she wasn't going to do it. This was around the time I was being accused by Group W of soliciting people not to guest-host. So I told her, "Char, thank you very much, I appreciate it, but you have to do what's right for Char."

Still, out of loyalty to me, she decided not to host the show. "By the way," she added. "I've been meaning to talk to you about what's going on, and to ask if you'd like me to do a reading for you. Right here on the phone."

"Okay, fine," I said. I was bored, it was late at night. I figured what the hell.

She said this little blessing to keep out any evil spirits,

and then started naming names. She's an alphabet psychic, which means she pulls letters out of the air, and let me tell you, she pulled out some real doozies that night. Cornell, for instance. There's a real unusual first name. She also knew that Cornell was a woman, and an attorney for Group W. She told me not to trust this woman. "Tell me something I don't know."

She also got their New York attorney's name, which hadn't been in the press, and Gregg's name, which I don't believe had been published either. Trust *him,* she said. Yeah, yeah, that I know. And as I began to nod off she said, have I ever talked to you about your mother? *That* woke me up.

"She's dead, right?"

"Yes."

"She wants to apologize to you."

"For what?"

"Was your relationship with your mother anything at all like your relationship with Group W?"

"Exactly. Everything was always my fault."

"Well," Char said, "your mom wants you to know that she's sorry. She couldn't help herself. Was she ever sexually abused as a child?"

Now I was starting to get the oogie-boogies. I think my mom and I talked about this maybe twice in her life, and I always went, yeah, right. I thought it was just mom fabricating stories, something she was quite good at. I can't imagine how Char could have gotten *this* from anyplace.

"Yes," I said, "supposedly she was."

"Now, who is William?"

"Her father."

"Was that who it was?"

"No."

"Her brother?"

"I don't think so."

"Does he have a funny name?"

"The only name I ever knew him by was Stoney."

"And this was a half-brother?"

"Yes."

"Well, she was sexually abused by someone close to Stoney and carried it with her her whole life. She just wanted you to know she's sorry if she passed any of those feelings on to you."

Mom? Wanted me to know this? Now? But mom was as dead as Marley on Christmas Eve. *Wait a minute! Mom had passed away just as Derk was coming into my life.*

It couldn't be.

Could it?

Aww, no . . .

*Mother always said I'd be
  very attractive*
When I grew up
*Different she said, with a
  special something*
*And very very personal
  flair*
*And though I was eight
  or nine*
I hated her!
*Now different is nice but
  it sure isn't pretty*
*Pretty is what it's
  about . . .*
*And everyone is beauti-
  ful at the ballet*

The Lawrence family in 1964.
Mom, Joni, Dad, me.

$\mathcal{M}$iss Fireball

Mother loved to tell me I was born with a clubfoot. Her favorite thing to say to me whenever she thought I was acting like a rotten child was that she should have left me in a wheelchair. An extremely delightful thing to say to your child. I have never, by the way, found any proof, either in my baby book, early photographs, or doctor's reports that I ever actually had a clubfoot.

Having had two children of my own, I know that a lot of things can happen when you give birth, a foot may be turned this way, a knuckle or elbow may get squashed, but they all usually sort themselves out. However, mom insisted until the day she died my clubfoot was so hideous she never expected me to walk. For years she used to say to me, "Stand up and look at your feet and look how badly one foot pronates!" I'd look and say, I do have fallen arches, maybe, but that's all. However, she insisted it was a clubfoot, and that I even wore a brace for a while.

She kept to that story for the longest time. When it no longer had the kind of impact she wanted, she'd get on the phone and threaten to send me to an orphanage. She would actually pick up the receiver and pretend to have these lengthy conversations about whether they could take me or whether they had any room for me.

I remember when I started dancing lessons going to see Maria Tallchief in *Swan Lake,* and thinking she was the most incredible thing that ever lived, and wanting to be a ballerina just like her. I had a little ceramic statuette of her I used to stare at on my shelf as I would go to sleep at night. Clubfoot or no, motherless or otherwise, I wanted to *be* Maria Tallchief!

I am an official baby-boomer. My parents, Howard Axe Lawrence and Nettie Alene Loyd, were married in 1945 and I was born at Cedars of Lebanon Hospital in downtown L.A., before the hospital moved to Beverly Hills. Dad's mother, Anna, was from Kansas City, his father, Simon Axelrad, an Austrian Jew who immigrated to this country at the age of seventeen. Dad went to court and had all of our last names changed when I was four years old. He became Howard Axe Lawrence. The law requires you to submit the reason you want to change your name. He said it was because everyone was always getting it wrong, Axelrod, Axeldorph, Axelgrease. So, as far back as I can remember, I was Vicki Ann Lawrence.

Dad's mother was a Christian Scientist, and that's how he was raised. He lost both of his parents years before I came along. It used to crack me up when we'd have dinner parties for Christian Scientists. I can't tell you how many times one of them would come into the kitchen, take me aside, and say, "Don't you have any booze in the house at all? Not even cooking sherry?"

Dad was born in South Dakota. He learned to play trumpet in high school. He came to California in 1937 on vacation and never went back. He graduated from UCLA with a business degree and a major in accounting. Among his college accomplishments was marching in the Rose Parade. Apparently he was late, and the gym was already locked up. He couldn't get his trumpet, so they strapped a tuba on his back, which he carried for five and a half miles up Pasadena Boulevard. Mom used to tell me, "Your father nearly went on the road with Glenn Miller." I figured maybe that was my show biz legacy. Only recently, when I was finishing up this book, did dad tell me, "Nope, actually I was in the accounting department at the Palladium where Glenn Miller was booked, and the offer was not to play in the band but to be their advance man." His musical prowess is now confined to blowing the bugle on New Year's Eve.

Dad was in the air force during World War Two. He went all over the world as an Accountable Dispersing Officer. In June 1944 he was stationed in St. Louis, where he met my mother. She was an instructor at an Arthur Murray Dance Studio. She always said they met on a blind date. "Nope," dad says, "I picked her up at a bar." Two months later they were married.

Mom's entire family was from Missouri, right close to where Thelma Harper lives. Coincidence? I think not.

I attended Woodworth Elementary School, Monroe Junior High, and Morningside High School, all brand-new institutions built along with the fast-rising postwar land development of Inglewood, just south of Hollywood. It was a new neighborhood when we moved into our home on Third Avenue, one that rose quickly and fell with equal speed. The year after I graduated from high school, the first barbed wire went up around the school grounds.

Then came the iron gates. I learned how to drive at Hollywood Park before "The Fabulous Forum" was built. Unfortunately I can't go back there today to revisit the site of my childhood, or show my own children where I was raised. It's too dangerous in anything but a helicopter.

During my junior year in high school, there was one incident of random violence. Today there's one every minute. It happened during cheerleader practice. The football team came in and one of the boys said, "When you girls are ready to go home, let us know, and we'll walk you."

"Oh," we said. "Aren't you nice. What's going on?" They told us there had been a stabbing in the girls' restroom. The victim died while in the hospital, and our class yearbook was dedicated to her. For me, it marked the beginning of the end of the neighborhood. It was a sad thing to watch.

I was five when my sister, Joni, was born. I don't remember us ever being close. Our lives were always on separate tracks. I vowed way back then, if I ever had kids, I'd have them close together.

At the age of eighteen, just after I started working on *The Carol Burnett Show,* we moved to an apartment in Hollywood. My parents had bought a lot up in the Hollywood Hills, part of the Doheny Estates, and during construction of our new house we lived nearby in an interim two-bedroom apartment.

It was close quarters for us. Joni was only twelve when we moved, and thrown into the Hollywood school system. As a result, she fell in with a much wilder crowd than I had grown up with in middle-class, conservative Inglewood. Every other day we'd wind up screaming, yelling, fighting, and tearing each other's hair out, mostly because we were forced to share a bedroom.

To get Joni out of that environment, my parents enrolled her in a series of private schools. The first one was in Beverly Hills. I took my first Carol Burnett show tax refund, two thousand dollars, and contributed it toward tuition for Joni's enrollment at Principia, a private Christian Science high school located in St. Louis.

*M*om and I liked to go shopping together, and I'd always help her around the house. My lasting memory of being with her in the kitchen is me setting the table, tossing salads, and after dinner putting the dishes in the dishwasher. I don't remember her ever teaching me how to cook.

Mom taught me the worst eating habits in the world. My favorite sandwich when I was growing up was white bread with butter and sugar, with the crusts cut off. My favorite dinner was on Sunday night. The TV trays came out and we watched *The 20th Century* with Walter Cronkite, my generation's *60 Minutes*. Dad barbecued the steaks. Mom baked potatoes. Of course, I did the salad.

We always traveled during the summers, two-month-long journeys in the family car. One year we drove across country and did the whole eastern seaboard. Because we were Christian Scientists, we went and saw every single dig Mary Baker Eddy ever dug. One summer we did the 1776 tour—Jamestown, the little cobblestone streets, all of it. Another summer was the Black Hills, Mount Rushmore, and the Grand Canyon. Still another year we traveled up the West Coast, through the Sequoias, Yosemite, and the rain forests, all the way into Canada.

I remember a number of pets, although if they caused any trouble at all, mom would immediately get rid of them. My favorite was a tiny Boston bulldog I became great pals with. Unfortunately he had a weak tummy and would upchuck all over the house, so he disappeared. When I was in high school we got a miniature dachshund

I named Samantha, after the character on *Bewitched*. She loved to sleep in my big beach bag, and we were very good friends. She'd get excited when she'd see me and tinkle. She didn't last long either. The longest-lasting favorite pet I ever had was a parakeet, I guess because parakeets can go in a cage. Chipper loved me so much he'd sleep under my hair. He'd crawl up at night when I watched TV and fall asleep under there. I could feel his little body wobbling and put him back in the cage.

One of Chipper's favorite games was hide-and-seek. One night he hid, he didn't come when I called, I came around the corner. He came sneaking from the other side. We converged, and I stepped on him. I stayed up half the night holding him in my hands. Mom had me put him back in his cage and said, "He'll be fine. Look, he's balancing on his little perch." The next morning he was on the bottom of the cage. Dead.

Mom decided she would surprise me and replace Chipper with an identical parakeet. The next day when I came home from school, there was Chipper Two in his cage. I hated him!

I had a number of girlfriends at different periods when I was growing up. Nancy Simon and I were pretty close when I was little, until her family moved to Palos Verdes, which seemed to me like the far end of the world. I went to visit her once, and there was nothing there, besides her house. The big event that weekend was the discovery of a rattlesnake under her brother's bed. We had to evacuate the entire house until her father killed it. I never went back there again.

Nancy Hayes was another really good friend of mine. I met her because we lived on Eighth Place, and she lived on Eighth Avenue. As a result, our families always got each other's mail. I lost track of Nancy after we graduated from high school. She went to USC, and I went to UCLA. One night just after I started college I called her and suggested we get together, and do everything we used to do in high school, like going to Bob's Big Boy, and then the movies in Inglewood. I had already begun appearing on the Burnett show, and while we were eating, a little girl came up to our table and wanted to know if I was Vicki Lawrence and if I was could she have my autograph. I said yes, and signed her napkin. When the girl left, Nancy looked at me and said, "You've changed."

I said, "No I haven't."

"Yes," she insisted. "You have."

It then dawned on me for the first time that when something dramatic happens to you, as it did to me when I joined the Carol Burnett show, you do indeed change— *in other people's eyes.* Suddenly friends you grew up with begin to think you're too good for them, or that you no longer want to be around them. When you become a celebrity, you begin to find out pretty quickly who your friends are. I haven't seen Nancy since.

I had no real desire to be in show business when I was a child. The closest I came to anything that even resembled show business was visiting dad at the Max Factor building on Hollywood Boulevard, where he worked as a CPA. I used to love to pretend I was his secretary, make lots of noise on the adding machines and mimeograph in his office. Because of dad, I always had wonderful science reports, like "How Lipstick Is Made." I remember that one because it was when iridescent lipsticks were really big. They used fish scales to get that shiny look, and that made for a really cool science report.

My mother didn't work, but she always said when Joni and I were grown up and gone, she was going to donate her time to the Junior Blind Foundation, or someplace that would appreciate her, because we certainly didn't.

She did have one job for a while, when I was a teenager, for a local jeweler. Her assignment was to go downtown to the jewelry mart and pick out jewels. She became really knowledgeable about pearls and diamonds, and loved it. I don't know why she quit, but I do remember while she had the job it was the happiest I ever saw her.

I do have to credit mom with pushing me in the direction of show business. As far as the really nutsy stuff that eventually drove me away from her, that didn't happen until later, after the Burnett show and my first marriage. I do remember it beginning when I was sixteen, and a sophomore in high school. Mom, who was only forty at the time, came home one day and announced she had to have a complete hysterectomy. That was the "standard cure" for a lot of female problems back then, I guess. After, her doctors put her on tons of hormones, and she went completely nuts and never came back. Crying jags, severe depression, radical mood swings, all of it. I remember mom's doctor gravely talking to the family about mother's behavior, telling us we'd have to give her a couple of years to get "evened out," because this was a really difficult thing for her to go through.

She put on a lot of weight after the operation, and used to tell me the reason that one of our neighbors, Helen, got through the whole menopause thing without missing a beat and was still in such fabulous physical shape was because she had sons. The net result was that I wound up feeling guilty about just having been born, and worrying for the longest time about having a daughter of my own.

I carried variations of that fear until years later, when I had my son, Garrett, and surprise surprise I put on a lot of weight. I ballooned up to 202 pounds before I finally gave birth. After, out of sheer desperation, I went on that liquid protein diet, the one where *People* magazine kept reporting the deaths of people who drank that awful red stuff. The editors would call me every Thursday for a little update, to see if I was still alive. When I was just ten pounds from my goal weight, my doctor told me he wanted me to start working out. My goal should be, he said, to run an eight-minute mile.

Piece of cake, I thought, remembering that four-minute, thirty-seven-second mile trophy from UCLA that dad always put in my face. Al took me down to a high school track to try my first mile. He said it would be easier there, because it was a flat quarter-mile circle. I jogged the first lap, I walked the second, I dragged the third, and I kind of loped the fourth. It took me nearly fifteen minutes.

The first time I actually did an eight-minute mile, I thought I was ready for the Olympics. Now, no one ever did that kind of conditioning when I was growing up. I'm a firm believer that physical exercise is one of the most important factors in keeping mentally as well as physically healthy. Moral of the story? Mom never worked out, Helen played tennis every day.

Still, mom was the one who carted me to all the ballet lessons, tap lessons, jazz lessons, and piano lessons. She's the reason I know all the old songs from the forties. She's the one who got me involved in all those contests and pushed me up onto the stage. She's the one who brought me to those recitals. And she is the one who made me practice, practice, practice. I remember in the third grade being urged by my mother to get up in the Christmas program and sing "The Christmas Song." You know, *Chestnuts roasting on an open fire* . . . and hating her for it, because I was so shy. I stood in front of the whole class glaring at her, and I can still see her glaring back at me.

Still, for better or worse, it always seemed to be mom and me. She took me to dozens of stage plays. My mother is the reason I fell in love with Mary Martin. I remember when I was in the third grade she took me to see *Peter Pan,* and I cried at intermission. She asked me what the matter was, and I said I was sad because it was going to be over soon. I got the album and only then did I finally put two and two together and realize that Peter was a woman. Until then, I kept waiting for him to come and take me. I was crazy in love with this boy! When I found out it was a woman I was devastated.

We saw *Oklahoma!* together when Gordon MacRae did it, and my eighth-grade graduation present was a trip to Grauman's Chinese Theatre to see *West Side Story* the day after it opened. *South Pacific, Carousel, Mame,* you name it, we saw it.

When I started high school, the guy thing happened, and my mother went completely overboard. Maybe she feared one of them would break up our act, who knows, but whatever the reason, she became obsessed with manipulating all my dates. "You may not go out with so-and-so unless you go out with so-and-so" because she liked him better. There were serious repercussions if I didn't go out with a guy I didn't particularly like that *she* did.

For a recent Vicki show we found two of my old high school friends. One, Tom Teague, had been an on-again, off-again boyfriend while I was a cheerleader. Like most of my early relationships, this one could best be described as abrasive. After the show he said, "I never really got very serious with you because your mother made it pretty clear that you had a career to concentrate on."

I was surprised to hear him say that. I thought our relationship didn't work because I couldn't get a fire started. I distinctly remember saying to him one night, "Isn't this a sexy light fixture?" and him saying, "How can a lamp be sexy." Oh.

He was the kind of guy who would say, "Meet you at the corner and we'll walk to school together." If I got to the corner first, I'd wait for him. If he got there first he'd leave without me.

He used to say really rude things to me, like, "You don't care about our football team at all. The only reason you're a cheerleader is because you enjoy getting in front of a crowd and showing off." As I said, it was an abrasive relationship. On the other hand, maybe Tom was right.

It struck me when I saw him again after all these years, that his impression of me had been greatly influenced by my mother.

I remember having a crush on a guy in high school named Jimmy Marino, who was a bit wild. Mom, though, was absolutely in love with Norman, one of the school's top athletes. So the deal was, I couldn't go out with Jimmy unless I dated Norman. Now, Jimmy was cool. He didn't treat me like a slut or anything, took me in fact to an Andrés Segovia concert. Playing classical guitar happened to be a fantasy of his, and I guess he figured if he asked one of the campus sluts to go with him to see Segovia, they'd laugh at him.

Mom, though, was, as I say, in love with Norman, who just drove me nuts. At the time, there was a hit song, *Norman, ooooh, oooh, oooh, Norman, ooooh, oooh, oooh, oooh* . . . Great lyrics, huh? When I went out with him, everybody teased me by singing it.

God love him, I just couldn't stand Norman. Among his many dubious qualities, he was a shot-putter. One day, a huge banner came running by our French classroom window: *"Vicki, please come to the track meet, I love you, Norman!"* My French teacher said, "Vive l'amour! You're excused!" Fortunately, it was in the middle of a quiz, and I couldn't leave.

At cheerleading practice that day, we were all sitting around talking about one of our routines, when this put came rolling across the room and hit me in the leg. It was a missive from Norman, who wanted to know why I hadn't come to the track meet. *LEAVE ME ALONE!*

Years later, after I had married Bobby, my first husband, I ran into Norman on the streets of San Francisco, and God, he was big and gorgeous and swept me right off my feet! I thought to myself, What could I have been thinking back then? What planet was I on?

Miltown was my mother's generation's version of Valium, and a staple in our house from the time I was a child. One night I was visiting a boy at his house when dad called and said I had to come home right away. "Your mother's taken too many tranquilizers," he said, "and I'm not sure she's going to live."

Well, of course, I freaked. What really happened, I now believe, was that I was with a boy mom didn't like, and this was as good a way as any to end that date. I said goodbye and rushed home. I walked in the house and couldn't tell whether or not she had really taken any pills at all, or maybe just enough so that she was bouncing off the walls, coming down the hall looking very Sarah Bernhardt. I went and checked her bedside table, which looked like the prop man had been there. The Miltown bottle was open, a few pills were spilled on the table next to a glass of water, several were on the floor, all perfectly placed. This kind of setup always used to get to me as a child, until I figured out that mom liked to use her crazy act as a way to keep me in line.

I have to say it worked pretty well for a while. Whenever she had one of her episodes, it was always my fault. I spent a lot of my childhood apologizing to her for something I'd done, even when I hadn't done it. When Al and I got married, one of the first things he said to me was, "Will you please stop apologizing?"

And of course, I automatically responded by saying, "I'm sorry."

As for dad I just sort of remember him being there, but not really *being* there. If you went to him and said, "Dad, I told mom the sky is blue and she's insisting that it's pink," he would always say, "But your mother was here first, and your mother is my wife, and so your mother is right."

"But dad, the sky is blue."

"I don't care. Your mother is right. Because your mother is your mother."

One time mom and I got into a horrible quarrel over whether or not it was Stephen Boyd who played the bad guy in *Ben-Hur.* I said he did, mom said he didn't. I just wanted dad this one time to say to her, "Sit down and shut up, it was Stephen Boyd!" But he just wasn't that kind of guy.

Once when I was a youngster, mom, on a whim, cut her hair short and dyed it blonde. She went from looking like Ida Lupino to Marilyn Monroe in one day. Now, we were one of those families that always had that "Six P.M., everybody sit down and eat dinner" rule, because that was when dad got home from work. This night we all sat down at the table and dad didn't say a word about mom's hair. Instead, he asked her, "What's new?" Joni and I were dying! Finally, mom screamed at him because he hadn't noticed her platinum curls. When she finally calmed down he just said, "Sweetheart, I love you, no matter how you look." He was *that* kind of guy.

There was never much communicating with him. When my mother was still alive I'd call home, he'd pick up the phone, I'd say, "Hi dad, how are you?" he'd say, "I'm fine, I'll get your mom," and that would be the end of our conversation.

He did have one passion, and I must say, it was a great one. He had one of the most extensive *Time* magazine autographed covers collections ever, so much so that *Time* actually did a story about him. It still breaks my heart to think that he eventually sold it, rather than handing it down to the family. It's something I really would love to have. I can remember him going through major obstacles trying to get some of them signed. When the first astronauts made the cover, he mailed the same copy to each one of them. He had to mail it eight times to get all eight signatures. One time the FBI came and investigated us. Dad wanted the autograph of the king of Belgium. Apparently, the king was a little paranoid and wanted to know what crazy person in the United States was asking for his signature. Also, for years, we got Christmas cards from Duke Ellington. They would unfold and cover the entire living room floor.

I had signed up as a freshman for a cappella choir in high school, and was sitting in this huge room with a bunch of other students waiting for the choir director to show up, when this obnoxious kid came in, sat down with a tape recorder, and said, "This is what I did with my summer vacation." He turned it on, and said, "Here we are with Johnny Mathis at the Greek Theater." Some of the kids started asking him about it, and I heard him say he was in the Young Americans. I asked him about it, and he said there was going to be an open audition for singers, but warned me that to get accepted "You have to be really, really good." I looked at him and thought to myself, man, if he can do it, so can I.

The Young Americans was a nonprofit singing group made up of Southern California high school students. To get in it you had to have a B or better average, and be fairly gifted in music. There was an extensive musical test you had to pass before you were even allowed to try out. There were actually about sixty Young Americans, thirty of whom would go on the road while the rest were held as backup and occasionally rotated into the starting lineup. As a result, there was a lot of jealousy and competition in the group.

The auditions were held at the big Masonic temple on Hollywood Boulevard. There were tons of kids. I was moved from room to room, for each speciality. One for dance, one for singing, and if you passed the preliminaries, you then had to try out with a specially prepared piece for the director. It was a tough day, but I made it—I was accepted into the group, and boy was I excited!

From then on, I spent most of my off time in high school, including weekends, working with the Young Americans. Because we were students, all our tours took place in the summertime and over Christmas vacation. The first time I ever flew in an airplane was with the Young Americans. Mom was pretty good about letting me go and do whatever I wanted. One Christmas week we played the Circle Star Theater outside of San Francisco, with Johnny Mathis. One summer we played the Greek Theater with Henry Mancini, which at the time we all thought was really cool!

I loved doing vocals to Mancini music better than anything. Close harmony is my favorite form of singing. (One of my unfulfilled fantasies is to sing background for Earth, Wind & Fire.) We got to do all of his great themes, "Days of Wine and Roses," "Peter Gunn," "Dear Heart," "Charade," "Mr. Lucky," all of them. What a thrill for me.

The last summer I was in the group we made a film called *The Young Americans* that won the Oscar for best documentary before being disqualified on some technicality. As far as I was concerned, we'd won, and that was that.

For some of the time I was in the group I dated Dick Brown, a fellow Young American. His nickname for me was Grace because, I guess, he thought I didn't have a lot of it. The thing I remember most about him was that he used to write me letters, and the envelopes were always so beautifully inscribed. He had real talent that way.

Dick was a Mormon. Our relationship ended when he went on his two-year mission. He never spoke to me again. He was, incidentally, the first person who ever French-kissed me, and scared the shit out of me when he did. I didn't know what he was doing, and he wasn't very good at it. I'd have to describe it as horrible. His tongue was as big as a cow's. For the rest of the night I gargled every two minutes! My roommates got a huge laugh out of it.

I also sang with a lot of other musical groups in high school. I formed a little singing group, the Fourmost, and we actually got ourselves a couple of little jobs. Our choir director recorded a school album in which our best songs were included.

I was also heavily involved in the dance department. I did a lot of choreography for them, as well as for the cheerleaders. This was back in the days when we hand-made pom-poms. I had to lay the tissue paper out, and thank God my dad had a paper cutter so I could cut the thin strips. I would tape them to the center to make a handle. Then I had to hand-crinkle every one of those pieces of paper and there were hundreds of them. What a job.

It was my fault that all the song leaders at school signed up for summer camp up in Redlands. The counselors were all college cheerleaders, and I wanted us all to learn some cutting-edge cheering stuff. I remember coming back that fall determined to change the way we did things. We were now going to prance the way they did in college. Unfortunately, everybody hated me for it because I became a real slavedriver. I was voted best choreographer by my class and most likely to succeed. Hey, when they're right, they're right, what can I say?

With mother's encouragement, I entered lots of contests. Mom always discovered them first, like the Father's Day contest when I was eight, for which I had to write an essay, two hundred words or less, on why I loved my dad. There was an older winner and a younger winner. I won in the juvenile division. The prize was a chemistry set with which I nearly blew the house up.

I was the runner-up to Miss Inglewood one year. It was

ROVin' Around...
...with R. O. V

YOU PROBABLY saw in your Daily News of Wednesday the story about Vicki Lawrence, eight-year-old Inglewood girl whose letter about her daddy was selected one of 10 winners from thousands submitted in a national "Letters for Father" contest.

That story had an excerpt from Vicki's letter included in it, but I would like to reprint its full content, which I feel contains some good thinking to have come from a girl of eight years:

"THINGS I LIKE ABOUT MY DADDY:
"Everyone loves my daddy; he is so good to us. When he sets up the trains he always lets us play with them. When I know he wants to play with them. He just lets us take me places and when he takes me to the boats he always lets me drive the boats when I know he wants to do it. I think he's the best daddy in the world. In the summer he took me and my friends to the train station. It is a very long time. And we had a very good time there. And one time we went to Marineland on my birthday and it was very fun too.

"FUNNY THINGS ABOUT MY DADDY:
"My daddy is funny. Sometimes he tells us funny jokes. Sometimes he is cornie. He makes us laugh and he also laughs too at his jokes. My daddy likes to make us laugh with him.

"THINGS THAT ARE SAD ABOUT MY DADDY:
"My daddy gets bold (bawled) out sometimes for things he dus. But when it's over, it's much better, cause when he gets bold out it's very noisie."

THOUGHT FOR FATHER'S DAY—When I was six or seven years old, I came across a poem that I liked well that I remember it to this day. It goes like this:
Never make fun of adopted kids,
Whether they're homely or not;
Always remember, their folks picked them,
But yours had to take what they got.

It's a common sentiment on Father's Day greeting cards to note that while none of us had a choice of fathers if we had had such a choice, we would have picked, from all the rest, our own Dad.

But on Father's Day I like to reverse this thought the little poem quoted above indicates, and thing along this line: as a continuing Father's Day gift for Dad, maybe I've that if my father had his choice, among all the others in the world, he would still pick me for one of his sons.

a beauty thing, and the winner was well connected. However, Miss Fireball, which I entered in 1966, my senior year of high school, was something else.

It was mom, again, who got me involved. The annual Fireman's Ball was coming up. Do firemen still have balls? Anyway, the neighborhood fire department wanted some bimbos to sing and dance for them, so they rented one of the large indoor rooms at the Hollywood Park racetrack, called it a contest, and sure enough, I was one of the bimbos.

The year I entered there were eight contestants, and it was an 1890's firehouse theme. We had to do two can-can numbers and perform individually during the talent portion of the contest.

About two weeks before the contest, a local newspaper woman, Beverly Summo, began a series of articles on each of the eight girls who had entered the contest. In the one she wrote about me she happened to say that I "bore a striking resemblance to a young Carol Burnett," and ran a picture of me singing at a Young Americans rehearsal. The article also mentioned my parents and where we lived. When my mom read it she said, "You really should write Carol Burnett a fan letter."

When I was young I wrote everyone a fan letter. My walls were covered with autographed pictures of television stars, Miss Universe contestants, Johnny Crawford from *The Rifleman,* Clint Eastwood from *Rawhide,* Shirley MacLaine, Peter Brown, Robert Conrad, Connie Stevens, Fabian, Ed "Kookie" Byrnes, you name it. Taking a cue from my dad, I had gotten into the habit of writing to everybody I liked, asking for their autographs.

At the time that mom told me to write the letter, I can't really say that I was an avid Carol Burnett fan. I don't even remember watching her on TV all that much. What I do remember is that from the day I entered high school, everyone told me I looked like her. The first time I sat down in history class and Joel Kuritsky walked down my aisle, he stopped and stared at me, then sat down behind me. A little later he tapped me on the shoulder and said, "You know what, you look just like Carol Burnett."

I looked at him and said, "Ah, well, you look like Abraham Lincoln." In fact, I thought he looked more like Lincoln than I did Carol! From that day on, it became a real thing at school. Everyone talked about our respective resemblances.

So, with mom's urging, I sat down at the kitchen counter and said okay, I'd write this letter. In it I said I was a fan of hers and hoped to meet her someday, and that everyone said I looked like her. I also told her I sang with the Young Americans and included the newspaper article.

Much later, I found out from her secretary, who was also her cousin, whom everyone called "Cuz," that Carol received the letter about two days before the contest. Cuz told me she used to sort out the mail, a lot of which wasn't all that readable, or from people who just wanted a signed photo. It was unusual to get a letter that actually had something to say, that was coherent and in proper English. Mine was one of about five letters Cuz handed Carol that week. She read it, got my dad's name out of the article, looked us up in the phone book, and called me up that day after school!

I was taking a nap, and I remember picking up the phone and there was no mistaking her voice. "Hi," she said in that funny roller-coaster pitch of hers, with all the words sounding like they were in italics, *"This is Carol Burnett."*

At first I thought it was a joke someone at school was playing on me. The spring musical happened to be *Once Upon a Mattress,* which Carol had starred in Off-Broadway and on television. Everyone had assumed that because of our resemblance, I was going to play the lead. In fact, I didn't have time to do it because I was so heavily involved in the Young Americans and the Miss Fireball contest.

So I asked who it really was on the other end, and again she said, "Carol Burnett." When I realized it was actually her, I froze. I handed the phone to my mom, to whom Carol said, very politely, "I don't want to talk to you, I want to talk to Vicki. Tell her she doesn't have to talk, all she has to do is listen."

I got back on and Carol said she wanted to come and see this contest that I was in. She told me she was very pregnant, and would prefer not to be seen, so if I could get her two seats way in the back that would be great.

My first reaction was, the woman must be out of her mind! That night, I went to the Miss Fireball rehearsal and asked the person in charge of publicity if he would re-serve two seats, *way in the back,* for Carol Burnett, and to please not tell anyone.

"Yeah, right, sure hon."

"No, really," I insisted. "Carol Burnett is going to come to the contest. And please don't tell anybody."

Right up to the night of the contest, I was excited and nervous wondering if she was really going to show.

Well, she did. She arrived in this huge, red cape and butt-ugly black turban with those famous red bangs hang-ing down her forehead. Very incognito, right? She and her husband, Joe Hamilton, sat in the back and watched the contest. This was the first time I'd ever laid eyes on Joe, and I remember thinking that he was just gorgeous, to die for! Man, I told myself, did she get lucky!

The contestants did the can-can numbers, and when it was time for my individual talent, I sang and played the guitar and the kazoo, which I wore around my neck. Af-ter, the fellow who had promised not to tell anybody about Carol, got up on stage and said, "I have an an-nouncement to make. We have a very special guest in the audience tonight." Now I'm thinking, "Oh, no, this guy is going to blow my entire career before it even gets started!"

He introduced Carol and said, "Would she be kind enough to come up on stage and crown the winner?" Great. As it turned out, Carol was very sweet about the whole thing. She came up, and did crown the winner, *moi,* thank you very much. Of course, none of the other girls would speak to me at all, figuring the whole thing had been a setup from the start.

Carol, who looked like she was twelve months preg-nant, crowned me with this big gold fire helmet, and just before she disappeared said to me, "I promise I will call you in a couple of weeks, we'll have lunch and discuss your career."

Carol had just finished a series, *The Entertainers,* which had been based in New York, with Bob Newhart and John

MISS FIRE BALL title winner during the annual Inglewood Firemen's Association ball November 26 was Miss Vicki Lawrence—being "crowned" with a gold fire helmet by Carol Burnett while Mayor William Goodike watches. The ball attracted a record 1,500 persons to Hollywood Park Turf Club as it was staged for the sixth time. (Another picture on page x.)

Davidson, whom she had also helped get started in show business. What I didn't know was that she was coming to the end of her contract with CBS. She had an option to do a series but had to come up with an idea. It was at that point that she and Joe decided to move out to Los Angeles to try and put together a West Coast–based variety show. As I remember Carol telling me later, she and Joe approached CBS with the idea for *The Carol Burnett Show* one week before her contract was scheduled to run out.

Among the first ideas they had was a "Carol and Sis" segment, to be loosely based on her early years in New York when she was married to her first husband, a struggling actor, and they took her kid sister in to live with the two of them. The sketch, as Carol always described it, was intended to be a recurring Ozzie and Harriet version of what was actually a much grimmer time in her life. They were looking for someone to play Sis, when, on a whim, Carol told Joe that she had gotten this letter, and had a feeling about the kid who'd written it. Joe asked where Carol was going to see me, and when she said Hollywood Park, he wanted to know if I was a jockey!

One day, a couple of weeks after the Miss Fireball contest, mom said she had heard on the radio that Carol was in St. John's Hospital in Santa Monica, where she'd given birth to a baby girl. I was recording an album with the Young Americans for the Firestone tire company. They used to put out a Christmas album every year, and we were the backup singers for this one. When the boy I was sharing a ride with to the studio picked me up for rehearsal that afternoon, I asked if he would take me to the hospital. I figured I'd just drop in and pay Carol a visit. My friend said, "You can't get in to see Carol Burnett."

I said, "I can try. I'll get some flowers and I'll use her married name, and they'll think I know her."

We arrived at the hospital, I went straight up to the maternity ward and saw two nurses sitting at their station looking quite bored. I walked up to them and said, "I'm here to see Mrs. Hamilton."

One of them jumped up and said, "Oh my God, you must be her sister, Chrissie! Wait'll you see the baby!" They ushered me right into her room, no questions asked.

Carol was surprised to see me, and very nice about my visiting her under such circumstances. "I haven't forgotten you," she said. "I promise I'm going to call you as soon as I get my tummy back. *I promise.*"

A couple of weeks later, barely into the new year, 1967, Joe called me at home and asked if I knew where CBS—"Television City"—was, on Fairfax, next to the Farmers Market. I said I did, and he told me he wanted me to come down there to his office to talk about a new show he and Carol were involved in.

That same day I met with Joe and Arnie Rosen, the supervising producer, and they asked me if I would consider auditioning for the role of Sis. I actually wrestled over whether or not I would, because just trying out meant having to give up my summer tour with the Young Americans.

The audition was scheduled for June, right when the tour was scheduled to start. I sat down with the director of the Young Americans and he said to me, rather sternly, "You need to understand something, young lady. If you decide to go and do this audition, and really, Vicki, what are the odds of it turning into anything, and you're not here for the beginning of the tour, and I replace you, I am not going to kick someone else off to make room for you."

It was a difficult decision to make. I was only eighteen years old, and auditioning for Carol meant having to say goodbye to all my friends in the Young Americans.

Joe later claimed he talked to hundreds of girls for the part of Sis, but I don't know if that's true or not. Reporters used to cross-examine Carol and me all the time, because they were convinced we had fabricated the whole story of how we met to make it seem like some version of the Lana Turner at the counter of Schwab's myth. One day during an interview Carol told a reporter the really interesting thing about the whole deal was that about a week after the Miss Fireball contest, her manager, Marty Goodman, happened to catch *The Andy Williams Show* that the Young Americans had done. He picked up the phone, called Carol, and said, "I'm sitting here watching TV and I have found the girl to play your sister. She sings in the Young Americans and looks just like you."

And Carol said, "That's Vicki Lawrence. I already met her."

The first time I heard her tell this story, I went, whoaa, that really is spooky. And then I realized that one way or another, Carol would have found me. It was just meant to be. The last time she was on my show I said to her, "If it wasn't for you I wouldn't be sitting here."

She disagreed. "Yeah, you would. It might have happened a different way, but you'd be here."

I do know at the time they had narrowed down their choice to me and one other actress, Heather North, a typical blonde, adorable, perfect teenage "actress."

I decided to do everything in my power to make myself look as much like Carol as I could. My natural hair color is mousy brown. I got some Lady Clairol No. 33, "Flame," dumped it on my head, and to this day, people still ask me if I'm a natural redhead.

The girl that has been doing my color for a number of years in Long Beach said a woman came in the shop about a year ago and wanted to be a redhead. Carolyn patiently explained how there are a lot of different shades of red. The woman then said, "I would like my hair to be the color of Vicki Lawrence's, but I know that's impossible because hers is natural."

I raised one eyebrow. "Well, Carolyn, what did you tell her?"

She smiled sweetly and said, "I told her I think I can do that."

For the longest time, the Redhead Club of America kept trying to present me with a lifetime membership. When I finally told them I was really flattered but I wasn't a natural redhead, they were stunned!

When I first moved down to Long Beach, I had to find all new doctors. For any woman, finding a new gynecologist is always traumatic. You know, of course, a man designed all those weird instruments, and what's the story with those stirrups? I don't know whose foot that's supposed to fit. They put you out there on a piece of paper buck naked, and . . . it's a very uncomfortable experience. During examinations, I always try to talk about things that are far and away from what's going on, to make light conversation, as it were. So when I found my new gynecologist, and I was, pardon the expression, laid out, we started talking about sunscreens. While he was down there doing whatever they do, he said, "Of course, you have very sensitive skin because you're a redhead."

I thought to myself, where the hell is this guy looking? Whatever he's doing, he's doing it with his eyes closed!

Anyway, remember the audition? They decided to shoot the same sketch twice, with each of us, Heather and me, playing Sis opposite Carol. I remember the day of my audition, I walked into the studio and as I was signing in, some big-time CBS executive grabbed me from behind, and kissed me on the neck! I turned around and he said, "Oh God, I thought you were Carol!" The stage manager then directed me to my dressing room and I accidentally walked into Heather's, where there were so many flowers it looked like somebody had died. Flowers, cards, balloons, and guys in suits.

I said, "Oh, I'm sorry, I must be in the wrong room," and went down to my little room, which had absolutely nothing in it. No flowers, no frills, no men in suits, nothing!

They taped each of us, wished us both good luck, and that was it, I was out of there. Two weeks passed before I found out if I'd actually gotten the role, during which time I was a nervous wreck. Then one morning, Joe Hamilton's secretary, Charlene, called. "Vicki," she said, very seriously, "Mr. Hamilton would like to speak to you."

Oh God, I thought, they were going to try and break it to me gently. He got on the phone and said, "We've decided that what we're going to do is . . . we're going to give you the role."

I couldn't believe it! Just like that, I became Carol Burnett's "sister" and my life changed forever.

*P*erhaps not coincidentally, this was about the time when things really started unraveling for mom. I found out years later from one of the secretaries that the day I auditioned for the show mom had called ahead to tell them to please be patient with me because I was having my period and could be very difficult. God, I thought, why would she do that? Looking back, I guess mom was jealous of everything I did. Especially my success. This, in spite of the way she had always pushed me in the direction I wound up. I'm sure it had something to do with the fact that she was a woman who didn't get to do it herself and that she deserved it, felt it all should have happened to her, and when it happened to me, it made her a little crazy.

As I said earlier, when my sister, Joni, was thirteen she went through her own set of problems. She was into a heavy period of rebellion, and maybe, like mom, a little jealous over my good fortune. And I wasn't around a whole lot to try to defuse it, even though I was still living at home, and continued to do so for the first few years the show was on the air.

Why? Because my mother had hammered it into me every day of my life that the new home they were building in the hills was for me, so I couldn't possibly leave. I always wondered why mom didn't think of it as something for dad, who worked right down the road, on Hollywood Boulevard, and who, until he'd built the new house had to schlep all the way from Inglewood every day. Why build a home for me when I was all grown up?

As I mentioned earlier, we moved into an interim apartment while the new house was being built. One day I came home from UCLA and mom was upset about something. I don't remember what the specific issue was, but like a scene from *Harold and Maude* she took a butcher knife from the kitchen and threatened to kill herself. She went storming into the bathroom with the knife and slammed the door. Joni started crying hysterically, but I rolled my eyes and said, "It's just mother."

Joni, however, wouldn't stop screaming and crying, so finally I went to the bathroom door, banged on it and said, "Mother, open up." There was no answer, so I said, "Mother, if you don't open the door I'm going to have to break it down." I knew I couldn't break any doors down, and so did she. You have to be a policeman or a fireman to be able to do that kind of thing. Still, I continued my bluff. "Mom, if you don't open the door by the time I count three, I'm coming in!"

I started counting. "One . . ." No answer. "Two . . ."

"What are you going to do," Joni whispered.

"Three . . ." I had no idea. I picked up my foot and jammed it through the door. Turned out, it was a flimsy apartment bathroom door, not very substantial, but who knew? Anyway, I reached in, unlocked the door, turned the knob, swung it open and there was mom sitting on the toilet, outraged at this invasion of her privacy. The knife was lying on the sink counter.

"What are you doing, mom?" I asked.

"I'm trying to use the bathroom. Do you mind?"

"What's the knife doing in here?"

"I am planning to fix dinner as soon as I'm through, if you will please leave me alone!"

Well, I felt like an idiot. Of course she had no intention of doing anything. The whole episode was prime mom. She had this uncanny ability to twist everything that happened so that I always wound up asking myself what the hell was I thinking? *Of course* she was going to fix dinner.

Anyway, the next day, I found mom out by the building's swimming pool, sitting on a lounge chair and talking to the manager of the building, explaining that her daughter Vicki had been so upset she'd broken the door down, that she was an actress, very high-strung, and that she would, of course, pay for the damage.

Shortly after we moved into the new house, I had an interview scheduled with a magazine about my role on the Burnett show. Mom suggested we do the interview at home.

All I remember about it is that I spent the entire time running for coffee, getting more cookies, going to find a certain picture, while my mom talked to the interviewer. When I finally finished my "errands" and came into the living room, mom turned to me and said, "Vicki, would you go and check on dinner, honey?" I don't believe I ever did get to actually talk to that fellow.

Mom used to tell me that when she was twenty-two years old she sang in a local band in St. Louis; mom and three guys. It had been their dream to run off to New York and hit the big time. One reason she didn't was because her mother put her foot down and insisted mom wouldn't be a show business bimbo. She used to love to lament with me about how awful it was that she never got her chance.

Unfortunately, mom was one of those ladies like so many from her generation who weren't allowed to pursue their dreams. Most of us female baby-boomers cannot turn around to our mothers and say, "How did you cope with all of this?" because, quite frankly, most of them didn't. They stayed home, baked cookies, raised babies, and became members of the PTA, always as Mrs. somebody. Women in my generation are sort of pioneers.

I guess the problem is worse with classic stage mothers, because they become jealous of whatever success their children achieve. Especially when their children leave them at the altar. For the parent, all the action is in getting there. Once I made it, the thrust of mom's frustrations were always the same, that it should have been her.

But it wasn't her. It was me. And my dreams were just beginning. No one promised the trip was going to be easy.

CHAPTER THREE

The original cast of *The Carol Burnett Show*.
L to R: Harvey, Carol, me, Lyle.

From Seaweed to Sis

I graduated from high school that June at the age of eighteen, and the following fall started my college career at UCLA and began working on *The Carol Burnett Show*.

My salary was union scale, something like three hundred sixty dollars a week. My uncle Irving looked over the contract and told me it wasn't that great a deal, and I said, yes, I know, but who am I? If I went to them and asked for more money they'd probably say screw off, we can always get another child actress off the street with no experience. It wasn't as if I had a lot of bargaining power. So I signed it.

I could take huge salary jumps every year forever and still not come even close to what Harvey Korman, Lyle Waggoner, and later on Tim Conway were making. By the end of the show's run, I had been with every major talent agency in Hollywood. No matter where I went, every time I tried to get a raise, the answer was always the same. I needed to be patient, my time would come.

I eventually landed at William Morris, where my agent was the soon-to-be-legendary Mike Ovitz. I was crazy about him and believed I had finally found the agent of my dreams. Someone to take me under his wing and make things happen for me. I always looked forward to his visits to the set, often accompanied by his young trainee, a fellow by the name of Michael Eisner. Just before the start of the show's seventh year, Mike said to me, "We're going to hold out for a better deal." As the start-up date approached, he'd say, "Not to worry, I've got this under control." We were set to resume taping the following Monday. Late Saturday night I got a call from Mike telling me I better have my ass in on time Monday morning or they were going to fire me. Well, I thought, thanks a lot.

Later on I found out that he had been in the middle of making his big move out of William Morris to form his own agency, CAA, and taking his biggest clients with him. Joe Hamilton was one of them. Unfortunately, I was not. As a result, I got caught in something I wasn't even aware was happening. When I called to speak to Mike a week or two later, the switchboard at William Morris politely informed me that he didn't work there anymore. No word, no forwarding number. *Nada.* The next time I saw him at CBS, I was so heartbroken I couldn't even speak to him.

Before Mike, I had tried one time to negotiate with Joe myself. One lunch hour during the show's fifth season I worked up the courage to ask if I could have a meeting with him, and he said, sure, come on in to my office.

I sat down and said, "You know, I really feel that after five years on the show, I'm finally pulling my weight and still underpaid. I think I deserve to make at least what Lyle's making."

Joe said, "Well, Vicki, Lyle is a man with a family to support."

I said, "Oh yeah, right, good point," and left. It took years before the bulb went on. When it did I said to myself, hey, wait a minute, what's a family to support have to do with anything?

Joe Hamilton was a "drinkin' Irishman," very cocky and very attractive until his later years when the booze and the cigarettes finally took their toll. And quite the ladies' man.

When I first started working on the show, I used to love to hang out in the control booth, the "cockpit" as we called it, a long glass-enclosed panel from where it was possible to look down onto the stage and watch the whole show come together.

I remember standing up there one day watching the dancers come on stage to rehearse one of their numbers. Joe was in the booth, looked down at one of the girls, and said out loud, "There's the next Mrs. Hamilton." I felt a stab in my heart. Here was a man, after all, beholden to a wonderful woman for pretty much everything good that had happened to him in his career, insulting her like that in front of her co-workers.

It got worse. Early on, I believe it was the second season, we were nominated for a Golden Globe Award. The night of the presentations, the show had its own table. Carol was supposed to be there but couldn't make it. She had gone to Boston to accept Harvard's Hasty Pudding Award, and was snowed in. So Joe, me, and the rest of the cast and producers went.

The night started off wonderfully, when I had the great fortune to meet one of the idols of my life, Fred Astaire. It had always been my dream to go across a dance floor with him. And now, here he was, sitting only a few tables away.

Since I wasn't dating anyone at the time, I had asked the lead dancer on the show, Don Crichton, to escort me to the awards. I whispered to Don, asking if we could go over and say hello to Fred Astaire. He said okay. I pleaded with him not to let me make an ass of myself.

Fred was so sweet. I interrupted him while he was eating, with his mouth full. I was such an idiot, and he was so gracious. He said (or tried to say) how lovely it was to meet me and kissed my hand, which I didn't wash for a week.

The awards were being given out the same night of the week our show aired. As a little surprise, Joe told us all that he was taping the show at his house and we were all invited back to his place after the awards to watch it.

After the last Golden Globe was given out, we all went out to the parking lot to get our cars, and as it happened, Don had a flat tire. He insisted on sending me along by myself, in a cab, assuring me he would get there as soon as the AAA came.

I arrived at the party by myself, and was promptly cornered by Joe, who was already pretty well drunk. The first thing he said to me was, "You know, Vicki, if you want to make it in this business, you're going to have to put out."

I was so young and naive I had no idea what he was talking about. Nor did I understand alcoholism. Neither of my parents were drinkers, and I wouldn't have my first drink until I was twenty-three, still several years away. Therefore, I couldn't recognize, let alone understand, that side of Joe at all. His remark caught me so off guard I didn't know what to do. And he kept badgering and throwing his arms around me whenever I tried to get away. Finally, he threw an arm around my waist and said, "This party is a fucking bore. Let's go upstairs, Carol."

Just then, thank God, Don arrived. He'd had a hideous time getting the tire repaired, and then got stuck in traffic. He took his coat off and made a beeline for the bar, but before he was able to get there I grabbed him and insisted that he take me home now.

"Can't I even have a beer first?"

"No," I said. "I have to leave right now."

Being the nice guy he was, Don said okay and drove me home. On the way, I told him what had happened. He wasn't very surprised. He'd worked with both Carol and Joe in New York for many years, and had gotten used to the drill. He turned to me and said, "Vicki, I know how upset you are, but you have to understand, this is pretty standard operating procedure with Joe."

"I don't understand," I said. "And I don't think you do either. How am I going to face him tomorrow at work?"

"Don't say a word," Don told me. "He won't remember a thing. Trust me."

I did and he was right. The next day, he acted as if nothing had happened.

That turned me off Joe. I no longer thought he was so attractive, and wondered how Carol could stay married to him for even one night. It still amazes me that Carol hung in there with him for eighteen years.

They first met in New York during *The Garry Moore Show* days when Carol was a featured performer and Joe was the producer. They fell in love and got married, the second time around for both. Carol inherited his eight kids, and they had three of their own.

Maybe theirs was a fairy-tale romance for a while. I don't know exactly when things went bad between them. I don't know what particular incident finally caused Carol to throw in the towel, but their divorce was painful for all of us who loved her. By the time they agreed to end it, they had nearly killed each other trying to arrive at a settlement, and I saw up close Carol go to hell in a handbasket. I could never understand what was so important that it was worth fighting over. One would think that when you reach a certain point, the simplest thing would be to simply divide everything up, say goodbye, and get on with your life.

Sadly, their divorce dragged on well into the run of *Mama's Family.* One of their worst battles was over ownership of those characters. As a result, for most of *Mama's Family,* which Joe produced, Carol and I simply didn't speak, I guess because I was working for the enemy. It wasn't that she was angry at me, or anything like that. She just didn't seem to want to have anything to do with anyone who had anything to do with Joe, and unfortunately that included me. All during that period I just wanted to grab her by the shoulders and say, "Give it up, let it go. It's not worth ruining your life."

When they finally did end it, it turned out that their business manager had been in cahoots with Joe, so Carol wound up fighting both men for her fair share. When you become successful, everybody wants what you've got, starting with your money. I learned so much from Carol about so many things, including, among other things, the essence of survival in a cutthroat business.

We taped *The Carol Burnett Show* as if it were "live," meaning that we stopped only for major screw-ups or unavoidable set changes. Carol had grown up in live television and liked to run her show the way Garry Moore had taught her. It was a massive weekly production, a self-contained one-hour original variety show. We used to do two tapings one day every week, at four-fifteen and again at seven-fifteen, and edit the best of both together into one show.

You could count the times we had to do pickups, or reshoots, on the fingers of one hand. For a variety of reasons, including expense and the present nature of television, there's really nothing like it on the air today. The last time we all got together was in 1993 for a network reunion special. During the taping, we sat around laughing and wondering how we were able to do it week after week.

• • •

s if all that wasn't enough for an eager eighteen-year-old, I also began UCLA that fall. I took every course that was available at seven A.M. The deal was, I could go to college as long as I was in the studio by ten. This was not an easy schedule to keep. I was usually on and off campus before the rest of the student body was even awake. Because of that, I had no traditional college life. For a while, I hung around the Theater Arts department. It was where Carol had studied, and since that's where I was headed, it was probably the best place for me as well.

There were, however, strict rules for theater majors that made it impossible for me to become one. To begin with, you had to audition for every play, and if you got a part, you were obligated to do it. Once you were in production, you had to be available every Friday and Saturday night. Well, that wasn't going to work for me. The Burnett show had its technical run-throughs on Fridays to set the cameras and lights and mark the performers' movements, and taped two shows on Saturdays.

UCLA also had a rule that for one quarter each year students had to do crew work, again on Friday and Saturday nights. So I pretty much wound up dodging the theater department for two years, until it was time for me to have to declare a major. It was one of those situations where someone would see me and start shouting, "Hey, you, you there . . ." and I'd disappear behind a corner. I became as clever at eluding authority figures as Richard Kimble.

Eventually, I went to see a counselor from the theater department to discuss my dilemma, and he told me if I couldn't make it in school, I'd never make it in the cruel world of the theater. I said to him, "But I'm doing fine in the cruel world of the theater, it's here that I'm not doing so hot."

I decided to talk things over with my favorite theater professor, who always wore a three-piece suit with watch fob, smoked a pipe, and taught theater history. The time had come for me to formally declare my major and I was thinking of dropping out, because it was becoming clearer to me every day I wasn't going to be able to do the show and attend theater classes full-time.

"If you want my advice," he said, "get yourself a notepad and sit in the empty audience at CBS every day and study the best teachers in the world. You are already where every other student in this department would give his or her right arm to be."

That was exactly how I felt, but hearing it from my professor somehow validated it for me, although I knew my decision to drop out was going to devastate my parents. I had no idea how I was going to break it to them.

To avoid the inevitable for a little while longer, I decided to stay on and major in dance, provided I could work out the right schedule. I went to the dance department, and because I was performing professionally, they agreed to be a little more flexible.

Dance 1-a was a basic requirement of the program. I showed up the first day in my leotard, threw my little duffel bag on the side of the room, sat down on the floor, and listened as the instructor, who had a crackly voice that sounded like Julia Child's, began the course by saying, "Today we will all be seaweed. Let us lie back on the sand, close our eyes, and feel that we are a piece of seaweed . . ."

As I lay there trying my best to feel like seaweed, I said to myself, didn't I do this when I was a freshman in high school? I had come prepared to do a traveling time-step, or perhaps practice my arabesque.

"Now, reach out and touch the piece of seaweed next to you . . ."

Fine, except the seaweed next to me weighed about three hundred pounds. She latched on to me and started rolling the both of us around, and I knew I was in trouble. When she finally let go, I quietly got up from the ocean floor, took my duffel bag, and tiptoed out of the class. That was my last day at UCLA.

I went home and told my mother I just couldn't do it anymore, that my schedule was impossible. Anyway, I said, if I was going to study dance, I'd rather do it in a professional class. I was already taking private jazz classes once a week from Bobby Banas, one of the original Jets in *West Side Story*. With that caliber of teacher available, why would I want to strive to be a clump of greens?

Still, it broke her heart that I was dropping out of UCLA. She'd never gone to college, and it had always been her dream that I would. It broke dad's heart too. He was a graduate of UCLA, and hoped both his girls would go there. To tell you the truth, before I joined the Burnett show, it had been my goal as well. I had had a whole other life planned for myself. I thought I would go to UCLA and learn how to be a dental hygienist, marry a rich dentist, and hang it up.

It seemed for the longest time people were telling me what a mistake it had been to drop out of school, although I could never quite figure out why. For instance, one time during the second season of the Burnett show, Garry Moore and Durward Kirby were guests, and I remember being lectured by Garry that I should have stayed in school. He told me about his two sons, one who had a Ph.D., and the other who dropped out of college and was making ten times more running restaurants on the East Coast. "So," I asked him, "what is it exactly that you're trying to tell me?"

He just repeated how important it was for me to stay in school.

Ah.

Anyway, freed from my schedule of classes, I did just what my professor suggested. I started hanging out at the

Burnett show during rehearsals, watching as they perfected their bits, listening to their verbal timing, seeing how what they did came together from the ground up. I'd have to have been a moron not to learn from those people, by osmosis if no other way.

Maybe four or five months later, I was walking backstage one day when they were changing the sets for a scene, stopped at the drinking fountain, put my head down and heard this deep voice behind me say, "I haven't seen you at UCLA lately." I turned around and there was my favorite theater professor, with a T-shirt on and a pack of cigarettes rolled up in one sleeve.

"My God, what are you doing here?" I was stunned!

"Well," he said, "I got to listening to what I said to you, and if you have to start from the ground up, that's where you start, and this is definitely the best place to do it." Sure enough, during rehearsals, there was my theater professor, moving sets!

*I*n the beginning, the only thing I did on the show were the "Carol and Sis" skits. The very first one I ever did, I had to come into the kitchen holding my books in my arms. In those days Danny Simon, Neil's intense older brother, was the show's sketch director. "Okay, kid," he said to me at rehearsal, "now come through the front door, throw your books on the sofa, head toward the kitchen, and say your first line," which was simply calling Carol's name. Easy, right? I came through the door, threw my books down, and was about to yell "Carol" when Danny shouted, "Hold it, hold it. *Stop!*"

"What's wrong?" I asked.

"Is that the way you come through the door when you get home? Is that the way you throw your books down?"

"I think so."

"Jesus," he said. "We got a lot of work to do here!" He took me aside lunch hour after lunch hour and worked with me on trying to look a little more "natural" and a lot less gawky. It took years to become unselfconscious, ungawky, and ungeeky on stage. Fortunately for me, because the show was an immediate hit, I got that time.

I'd find myself in those early sketches standing on stage doing three or four lines and then saying, "I'm going to Marsha's house." That line became a running joke on the set, because it was how they used to get me out of the

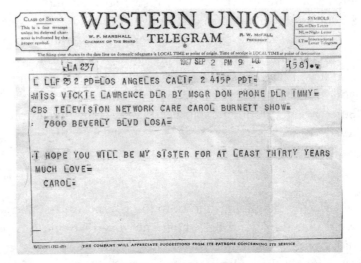

sketch. Every time I was on, I'd look out at the audience, at all the cameras in the studio, I'd see Carol and Harvey Korman and I'd say to myself, what the hell am I doing here? It was the weirdest sensation to have literally been plucked out of my life and into this place I'd never dreamed of being.

It wasn't until 1968, midway through the second season, that the producers felt comfortable enough to give me anything other than "Carol and Sis" sketches. It finally happened when I was asked to be in a takeoff of *The Newlywed Game,* with Lyle Waggoner as the host, Carol and Harvey one of the married couples, and one of our writers, Kenny Solms, and I another. Kenny, who was very nerdy-looking, played his character, complete with Nehru jacket and love beads. I was his bimbo wife, complete with a huge blonde wig and a squeaky, high-pitched little voice. It wasn't much of a part, but I imagine the thinking was if I could pull it off, I would get more to do on the show, and if I were horrible, at least I wouldn't screw up the entire sketch. As it happened, that little blonde bimbo character took off and became something of a staple for me on the show.

Early on, I became very close to both Harvey and Lyle. Lyle and his wife, Sharon, lived near the studio, so he'd often bring me with him for a home-cooked lunch. He kind of took me under his wing and taught me silly, fun things, like juggling, sculpting, and magic tricks. He, Sharon, and I became very good friends.

But it was from Harvey that I learned most everything I know about how to perform comedy. Once he saw there was an inkling of potential, he worked long and hard teaching me dialects, mannerisms, timing, and character development. Without any question, Carol was the one who gave me the first leg up. It was Harvey, though, who taught me how to ride.

I remember the first time I had to play an old woman. The sketch was a takeoff on all those thirties horror movies. Harvey played the proper English gentleman who sometimes has a problem when *the moooooooooon gets full* . . . After getting a flat tire, Carol shows up at the mansion with her boyfriend, played by Paul Sand, that week's guest star. I played the wicked old grandmother who appeared out of nowhere to explain to these youngsters how you go about killing a vampire. Harvey worked with me quite a lot on that character. In the script it said, "Vicki plays a Maria Ouspenskaya type." We got to the table-reading, and I said I had no idea who a Maria Ouspenskaya was! Everyone then said, as they always did whenever I didn't get it, "Oh Vicki, you're so naive."

When we got to rehearsal, Harvey said, "I think you need to make her Jewish." He started to work with me on developing the character as an old Jewish lady, complete with accent and mannerisms. He fixed the cane with props so that at one point I could leave and it would stay standing while I kept walking.

When Harvey was done with me, Maria Ouspenskaya was gone and I was left with a new character. I got a lot of laughs with my "*Wampire*" routine: "*You kill them with a stick, a stake, and a schtick!*"

Harvey is one of the best sketch comedians, especially when it comes to developing characters. One thing I always admired about him was that he would never say, "This sketch stinks, I hate this, I can't do this." Instead, he would say, "Let's make this work," and refuse to give in until the writers would throw up their arms, surrender, and say, "That's it, time out, we're cutting it, it's over."

One week Carol, Tim, Harvey, and I were in a horrible sketch we all hated. The writers, however, thought it would work and Joe insisted we go with it. It wasn't until the middle of taping, with the audience in place, no laughs, and us sweating bullets that Joe came through one of the set doors, walked right into the middle of the sketch and said, "Stop doing this!" Finally, a laugh!

It was the show's extremely good fortune to have Harvey on board. When Carol and Joe were still in the planning stage, they knew they needed a great leading man and a great character actor as regulars. Lyle came out of the audition process. They wanted a Rock Hudson type, hunky and gorgeous, and he was perfect for the job. Harvey was more difficult to find. They went through hundreds of names, until one day somebody in a meeting said, "You know what we need to do is find a Harvey Korman."

Carol then said, "Has anybody asked him?" *The Danny Kaye Show,* where Harvey had been a regular, had just left the air, and he could still be seen occasionally leaving the CBS parking lot. One day Carol stopped him and asked if he'd be interested in doing the show. The rest is TV history.

Carol always believed that she was only as good as the people around her. Her philosophy on the show was, the better they looked, the better she looked. Many people in this business do exactly the opposite. They want to be the top dog, and surround themselves with mediocrity because they believe it will make them look better. That doesn't leave very much room for real talent.

Carol was the kind of person who would say, "Vicki needs a new joke line on page seventeen." I'd be sitting there in the corner doing my needlepoint, and I'd say, "I do?" and she'd say, "Yes. Quiet." If you had a scene going well and she wasn't in it, she would be the first person out of her dressing room on the side of the stage leading the laughter. Harvey especially appreciated this, having come from Danny Kaye's show, where Danny would rework all his sketches so that he got all the funny lines.

Now, Harvey is one of those people you just love to hate. He is perhaps the most cynical person I have ever met in my life. His philosophy was, "Most of us are in this business because we're *fucked!*"

Thank you, Harvey. Let me get my needlepoint out.

I once did a show built around celebrities and their most influential teachers. Harvey was mine. I called to see if he would come by to make a special appearance. I figured he should be there. When I got him on the phone, his response was short, sweet, and to the point. *"NO! ABSOLUTELY NOT! LEAVE ME THE FUCK ALONE!"*

I called him three years ago when Carol was being inducted into the Television Academy Hall of Fame. There was a huge party, and I wanted to know if he was coming.

"How are you, Harvey?"

"How am I? I'm a neurotic old Jew sitting around in my caftan getting fat. What do you want?"

"I just called to see if you were coming to the academy," I said, in as tiny a voice as I could manage. He didn't come. I don't know what he's so mad about. Maybe he *is* a neurotic old Jew.

I learned early on that "old lady" characters are a mainstay of mine. I was only twenty-four years old when I first played Mama. Carol was originally going to play her right up until she read the final draft of the script and said, "I really think Vicki would be more suited to playing Mama than me."

Great, I thought. I get to play the old bat and she gets to be the ingenue. I guess that's how it works when the name of the show is Carol Burnett.

The character grew out of a sketch written during the show's sixth season by Dick Clair and Jenna McMahon, both of whom claimed they hated their mothers, and that the sketch was a kind of joint comic exorcism for them. They had adjoining offices. They'd write nonstop for days, then we'd hear them performing the sketch. She'd play all the female parts, he'd do all the males. We could hear them all the way down the hall. Then it would get quiet again, except for the sound of typewriters. They'd pick the sketch apart until, after maybe four or five weeks, they'd have one written.

Roddy McDowall was the guest star the week the sketch debuted. In it he played a Pulitzer Prize–winning novelist who had left his family to go off and become world-famous and was now coming home to visit. The family was ungrateful and thankless to him, as some families are when one member becomes famous. Because it was Roddy McDowall, who is so completely British, it never dawned on anyone that Carol would choose to do the sketch with a Southern accent. However, she saw it as a parody of Tennessee Williams. From the beginning she wanted it placed in Texas, somewhere around San Antonio, where she is originally from.

I was sick the Monday we began that week's rehearsals, and when I came in Tuesday morning Dave Powers, the show's director, asked me, "Do you think you can do an old person with a Southern accent?"

I said, "I'll try." We started working on the sketch and it all kind of fell together quite nicely. In addition to the cast, our costume designer, Bob Mackie, was, as always, invaluable to the realization of the piece. What a genius. I can't tell you how many times I didn't know where the hell I was going in a sketch until I went over to wardrobe, where Bob would put me in a costume that would instantly help define my character. With Mama, he built a soft round baby bunting "body" into a slip that I literally stepped into, zipped up, and covered with a lovely polyester frock, little old gray wig, round glasses, stockings mushed down under my knees, and old shoes. Once I was dressed like Mama I started walking like Mama, and before long *became* the head of this horrible, dysfunctional Southern white-trash family.

Run-throughs were on Wednesday afternoons, the first time the writers and the staff could see what we were doing. When Dick and Jenna saw what we had all done to their sketch, they threw their pencils and notepads down and stormed out of the rehearsal hall. Later that day they went to Carol and told her she was going to offend the entire Southern half of the country. But the sketch stayed the way Carol wanted it. We ended up getting so much positive mail that what was intended as a one-time thing became a recurring sketch. The writers still hated what we had done to the characters, but it didn't matter. As I said before, the name of the show was "Carol Burnett."

It didn't take long for "The Family" to become the most popular sketch on the show. In the seventies, false eyelashes were the thing. Carol and I both used to wear two sets of upper lashes and a set of lower lashes. We would get made up for the show and that was pretty much it. The first time I ever played Mama, I did it with these showgirl eyes. When the character took off and we knew it was going to be recurring, Al said I had to take two seconds to rip my lashes off, knock the rouge down and take the lipstick off. So it was that I became the only person in Hollywood who, when the cue was given to shoot, would go into makeup to get ugly.

Interestingly, after the Burnett show went off the air and Mama spun off into a separate series, there was a lot of talk about doing a major old-age makeup on me, to make Mama look more realistic. It was Al who said, "You cannot change that face that America has grown to love." And he was right, of course. Consequently, when people ask me how long it takes to become Mama, I tell them about five minutes. It takes me a hell of a lot longer to become Vicki.

*I*n those early days, I didn't really have much of a social life. I do remember the very first Hollywood party I went to. It was at Rock Hudson's house. I had just been cast in the show when Rock decided to throw Carol a big "Welcome to Hollywood" bash up at his home in the hills, complete with lots of big celebrities to help roll out the red carpet. Everyone had to park at the bottom of the hill, where a van was waiting to shuttle people.

Rock's home was beautifully lit and catered to the nines. I walked in, strolled by the bar, and the bartender asked me if I wanted a drink. I decided I'd better throw my gum out because I shouldn't be chewing it like a nerdy teenager at such a fancy affair. I casually tossed it in a nearby open bag and the bartender said, "Excuse me, that's the ice."

"Sorry," I said. "I've never been to a big Hollywood party before."

Carol's sister, Chris, was married to Will Hutchins, who'd starred in the old *Sugarfoot* TV series. I'd had such a crush on him (yet another autograph on my bedroom wall) and now I had actually gotten to dance with him! I also got to see Rock Hudson's bedroom (not with Will), and thought I'd absolutely died and gone to heaven!

Mostly, though, my socializing was confined to the immediate surroundings of "Television City in Hollywood," where I spent most of my waking hours.

I probably dated every usher at CBS. I also distinctly remember sitting in the empty audience one day and remarking to one of the female dancers that I was going to go through every one of the guys. We had about a dozen of the best male dancers in the business on the show, and I had crushes on them all. She looked at me and said, "Vicki, sweetie, most of them are gay."

I was devastated! "You mean him . . . and him . . . he is too?" What a rude awakening. It broke my heart in a million pieces! I had such plans! The best-looking guys, and the most fun of anybody—what a bummer! Once again, everyone thought, how naive can this girl be?

The answer was, very. I was still living at home, still a virgin, wet only behind my ears. But not for very much longer.

In Vietnam with Johnny and the boys.

Little Darlin' Baby Angel . . .

I lived at home for the first two seasons the Carol Burnett show was on the air. It wasn't until 1969 that I finally got my own little apartment. Sooner or later everyone learns to leave the nest. My time finally came when my mother made the nest no longer livable.

Sometimes on Saturday mornings my son, Garrett, sleeps until eleven. He's seventeen, and that's what you do when you're seventeen. I never had that luxury. Mom had an intercom system installed in the Hollywood Hills house, and her favorite thing to do was to turn it on first thing Saturday morning, so that there would be music blaring in my room whether I liked it or not. It was one of those systems where she could talk from the kitchen to whatever room she wanted, and she loved to do just that.

If I still didn't get up, she would vacuum right outside my door. I was keeping a very hard schedule at the time, between the Burnett show and school. After I dropped out, the pace kept up, because I did the summer replacement show with Jimmie Rodgers at the end of the first season. We went out and did location pieces for it, often worked into the night, and if I wanted to catch up on sleep Saturday mornings, there was just no way mom was going to allow it. I needed a little more privacy and a lot more space. Not to mention sleep. That's when I knew the time had come for me to fly.

I have always loved antiques. The first major purchase I made after landing the job with the Carol Burnett show was a brass bed with little roses for two hundred fifty dollars (I still have it, it's in my daughter, Courtney's, bedroom now). I absolutely adored it, because it's so hard to find brass beds that are feminine. To a certain extent, it also represented freedom to me.

I found it in the back of an antique store on Melrose Avenue. It wasn't very pretty, but the store owner assured me all it needed was a good polish, which, I found out, was not such an easy thing to do. My boyfriend at the time, Horace Heidt Jr., helped me, and it took us forever. It was, as I say, a very important purchase.

I also had a little secretary that I loved, and a few other pieces I wanted to take to my new apartment. Mother was upset about this. Not because I was moving out, but by doing so I was leaving one of her rooms undecorated.

The night before the big move I stayed at a girlfriend's house, and got up early to meet the movers, who were coming first thing the next morning. I remember it was drizzling that day and mom had put all my things out, uncovered, on the front porch. By the time the movers came, everything I owned was soaking wet. Thank you, mother.

My new apartment was on La Peer Drive in Beverly

Hills, between Wilshire Boulevard and Burton Way, not very far from either the studio or my parents' house. The symbolic distance was far greater than the physical.

It was a cute little place, not very spacious, a little one-bedroom with barely enough room for my brass bed, one bath, with a small kitchen and dinette. I crocheted an afghan for the foot of my bed. Mother used to come over regularly to "inspect" the apartment and would always say something like, "Vicki, you were never this neat at home." She was right. That's when I would try to explain to her that part of growing up was becoming neat when you got your own place.

I laugh about all this now because before Courtney went off to college, I informed her that when the stuff from her room actually started creeping out into the hall we would have a big fight. The cleaning lady still goes into Garrett's room, stands in the middle of the carnage and says, "Mrs. Vicki, I don't know what to clean . . ." I always use the same rule of thumb with the kids' rooms. If you can't see the carpet don't bother cleaning anything. That's their job. Of course when Courtney went away to school, the first thing she did was call me up and bitch about how sloppy her roommate was! *There is a God!*

Anyway, as a gift for graduating from high school, mom had given me my grandmother's gold locket. I have a photo of her wearing it. It was a very pretty piece of antique jewelry, and very dear to me. I took it to the new apartment with the rest of my pieces in the jewelry box. One day mom came over and out of the clear blue said accusingly, "Where's your grandmother's locket?" That's when I discovered it was missing.

I couldn't find it anywhere and didn't know what to say. I was sure I had misplaced it somewhere. After she left, I started to wonder if she had known it was missing all along. Later on, I found out from the building manager that she had come down one day, said she was my mother, talked him into letting her into my apartment, and took the gold locket. When I confronted her about it, she said she didn't think I was taking good enough care of it, leaving it unsecured right there in my jewelry box.

It was always a battle for possessions with mom. Things, that's what was important to her. Because the new apartment was so small, when I moved I couldn't take a lot of things with me. Among the many I left behind were two ceramic elephant garden stools from Vietnam. Mom kept them in the living room. Later on, when I moved to a larger place and asked for the elephants, and my big old armoire with lion's feet, mom flat out refused to give them to me. Those pieces had become part of her home, she said, and I couldn't have them back.

We argued periodically about them for years, until one day, not long before she passed away, she called me up and suddenly said, "You can have your armoire and damn elephants. Come and get them." Al and I talked about it. The elephants were some of the few things I had purchased in Vietnam. The factory that made them was blown up during the war. It would have meant a lot, but we decided it wasn't worth having them sitting in the middle of our living room because every time I'd look at them they'd remind me of the many fights I'd had with my mother over them. So I called her back and said, "You know what, mom, I don't want them anymore. It's not that important."

So she gave them away.

I bought the elephants while on a trip to Vietnam in 1968. The opportunity to go had come about after I'd been interviewed on radio by Johnny Grant, the legendary "Mayor" of Hollywood. In the sixties, he did a Hollywood-USO weekly radio show for broadcast in Vietnam. At the end of the interview, he said to me, "You ought to come on our next trip over there." I didn't even know he made trips. Or, for that matter, much of anything about the war at all. I wasn't very political, just a self-involved kid into doing my own thing.

As it happened, another girl had canceled out at the last minute from Johnny's upcoming tour. He usually took three girls with him, so he asked me to take her place. Johnny liked to take young girls rather than older stars, because most of the boys over there were still under twenty. It sounded exciting, so I said sure, if my mother would let me go, I'd love to. Johnny called my mom himself to get her permission. She got all the information, thought it over, and said yes.

We left right after I finished my first season of summer stock. I did stock because one of the most important pieces of advice Carol gave to me early on was that when the season ended I should get out and do it.

I asked, "Why?"

"Because," she said, "to put on a musical production in one week is nearly impossible, and it will be the best intensive training that you will ever go through."

I took her advice and wound up doing stock for years, and still do when I have the time. She was right, it was an incredible learning experience. I did things like *Carousel,* for the Kenley Circuit in Ohio, with John Davidson as my co-star. That's a difficult show to do in six months, let alone one week.

I developed a major crush on John. I got to talking with him about the war one day during rehearsal, and he said, "Vicki, I can't believe you're actually going there! You're such a bright girl. Why would you waste your time on that war?"

I said, "Gee, those guys probably don't want to be there either. Don't they deserve to see someone from home?" As I gradually discovered, resistance to the war in the show business community was pretty strong. Most people thought I was just plain nuts. Whoever I talked to had the same reaction: what the hell was I doing and had I lost my mind?

Prior to my actual departure, I had to sign dozens of re-
leases and take all kind of shots. At one point I had to
drive fifty miles to the Long Beach naval station to get
some exotic vaccine they didn't have anywhere else in
Los Angeles.

I was in Vietnam a total of three weeks during the summer of 1968. The tour was Johnny, me, Melody Patterson,
a young actress who was on *F Troop* at the time, and
Karen MacQuarrie, a runner-up in the Miss World pageant.

We flew to San Francisco and were held over at the
base for twelve hours before taking off for Saigon, with a
stopover in the Philippines. I remember that our commercial jet was filled with servicemen, and as we approached
Vietnam all the stewardesses strapped in and said, "Hang
on." It felt as if we landed literally straight down. And we
almost did. Pilots couldn't glide in low over the bushes at
the end of the strip because of snipers, so takeoffs and
landings had to be as swift and steep as possible.

Our first night in Vietnam we stayed in an old French
hotel in Saigon. We met our escort officer, "OB," short for
O'Brien, and everyone except me went out with him for
dinner. I was so tired, I just headed to my room and slept.
Or tried to. The Special Services officer had warned us
that if we heard any sort of incoming fire, we were to
grab the two straps on either side of our mattress and
bring it over on top of us as we fell to the floor.

"How will we know if it's incoming or outgoing?" I
asked.

"You'll know," he said.

The plumbing in the hotel was weird. The toilets would
flush themselves every hour on the hour. I'd wake up,
hear the toilet flushing, and a full minute would pass before I realized there was nobody there. It was pouring
rain, the thunder made the building shake, and the lightning illuminated the room. I didn't get much sleep that
night. The next morning, I said to the Special Services soldier, "That was some thunder and lightning last night."

He said, "Vicki, that was shelling. Like I told you, you'll know when it's incoming."

We flew on every aircraft imaginable, including General Westmoreland's personal Learjet, several C-130s, and double-boat Chinook helicopters. We all thought it was so cool to sit on the outside next to the gunners, who gave us a lovely tour of the countryside.

We went everywhere. Da Nang, Phu Cat, Cam Ranh Bay, Bien Hoa. We would fly around in helicopters all day visiting firebases. We got to this one place, somewhere remote, Phu Cat I believe, and I had to go to the bathroom so bad, our escort officer said, "Well, I'll just block off the latrine here, and you can go on in."

The latrine was just walls of cement blocks with the toilets lined up in the middle. OB stood at one end, no one thought about the other end. No sooner did I sit down when a soldier walked in and caught me in the act! He took one look at me sitting on the toilet, and to tell you the truth, I don't know which one of us was more embarrassed. There was nowhere for me to go, so I sat there staring at him, he looked at me, and he went running! Talk about getting up close and personal with the troops! I hoped I wouldn't see him the rest of that whole day, or, for that matter, the rest of my life!

We would go mostly to hospitals to visit the wounded. Johnny explained to us that they were the safest places because the enemy didn't know how many POWs we might have there, so they tended not to bomb the hospitals. We toured the wards at night, served dinner to the troops, slept in the nurses' quarters, got up in the morning, served breakfast, then flew out to area bases to visit more soldiers. Then it was off to another hospital for the evening.

We were supposed to leave Vietnam the eighteenth day, but because there was so much shelling going on around the airport, and so many more hospitals to visit, Johnny arranged for us to stay for three more.

I remember going to one hospital and seeing this beautiful little girl who looked about five years old that the soldiers had picked up in a deserted, burnt-out village. She had spinal meningitis, and the army doctors had performed surgery on her seven times, with several more scheduled. She didn't know a lot of English, except to say, "Me Number One," and "I love you." She hugged a lot too, and, oh dear, she knew how to do that so well. I had this long discussion with Johnny about taking her back to the United States. As you might expect, he was totally against this. Why, I kept wanting to know, couldn't I adopt her?

"Because you're nineteen years old, with no family, no husband, and you're out of your mind!"

Oh. But besides those reasons . . .

My impression of Vietnam was that it was one of the most beautiful places on earth. We would fly over lush, beautiful jungles, and out of nowhere come upon these spectacular waterfalls. I've never seen beaches like the ones in Vietnam. The sand was almost pure white. Midway through the trip we got a day off, went to Cam Ranh Bay, absolutely one of the most physically gorgeous places I've ever seen. All I kept thinking was, Hilton should just buy this country, set up camp, and end the war right then and there!

The troops at Cam Ranh Bay gave Melody, Karen, and me a little recon (reconnaissance) raft to use for an afternoon. The bay was so quiet and gorgeous. Even with little waves flapping we could see all the way to the bottom of the ocean. We were so exhausted, we all fell asleep for six hours on that raft. I'd never been in tropical sun before, I didn't know anything about sunscreen, and by the time we came in that night, I was so sunburned I looked black! And so sore I needed help getting dressed for days. I've had trouble tanning ever since. Before Vietnam, I was a little olive-skinned kid who used to put cocoa butter on, go lie at the beach, fry, and get a great tan. After, I got so many freckles, to this day I cannot take much sun.

A lot of bonding took place between us and the soldiers. I had special publicity pictures taken for Vietnam, and Johnny had them made into little postcards. I signed thousands of them, and shook countless hands. We were in the hospital one night and I met a marine pilot who had been shot down the day before who was all bandaged up and on crutches. He wasn't in terrific shape. He asked me whereabouts did I live in the States. When I told him right above the Sunset Strip in the Hollywood Hills he went crazy. "You live with your friends, those fucking hippies," he said. I excused myself and got out of there. I was all the way down the next ward when he came hobbling after me, broke down crying in my arms and apologized. "I shouldn't have said that to you, but I just lost my best friend. He was a conscientious objector and would not carry a gun, but came to Vietnam anyway. I'm a pilot in a medevac chopper. We flew together. His job was to jump out, grab the wounded, and load them in the chopper. He was killed yesterday."

It was amazing to me how many soldiers had actually wounded themselves just to get out of the war. I'd go over to one in a hospital and say, "You poor thing, what happened," and he'd start laughing and say to me, "Oh, I shot myself." They'd tell you how they just didn't want to be out there. They were so conflicted, because of official policy that told them, okay, you're here, but you're not allowed to do anything, the infamous "limited commitment" so many of the boys found impossible to understand, let alone follow.

I'm glad I went, and would do it again. Maybe one of the strongest reasons is precisely because they didn't have a lot of support back home.

Everybody remembers the Bob Hope Vietnam trips, and I think what Bob did was incredible. He'd fly in to the huge bases, do a show on a stage, and then fly back out, to somewhere like Thailand that same night. His troupe usually stayed in Bangkok most of the time. What Johnny did, however, was to go into the trenches. He'd get out to the little firebases no one else saw. Ours was a one-on-one handshake tour, not a prepackaged entertainment show. It was an intensely personal experience.

I came back from Vietnam with pages and pages of phone numbers. Everywhere I went guys would say to me, "Could you call my mother when you get back and tell her I'm okay?" Which, of course, I was more than happy to do. That fall, for two weeks every night after working on the Burnett show I did nothing but make phone calls to tell people I had just seen their son.

I did a *Vicki!* Vietnam reunion show with the girls who went with me to Vietnam, Johnny Grant, a houseful of veterans, and B.J. Thomas. B.J. was on because shortly before we were set to tape, I happened to receive a letter from a fellow who suggested we do a show about Vietnam veterans, and he wanted me to know that B.J. had saved his life in Vietnam.

The fellow was a huge B. J. fan and had taken all of his albums to Vietnam. He was captured, locked up along with three or four other guys in individual cells. In the dark, the boys would entertain each other by singing "Raindrops Keep Falling on My Head."

Years later, he was sitting at a truck stop near his home somewhere in Arizona, and B.J.'s bus rolled up. B.J. came in for coffee, and the ex-soldier went over to tell him this story about how that song had saved his life. B.J. in turn invited him to the concert that night. After the show, the guy gave B.J. his Purple Heart. B.J. didn't want to take it, he'd never fought in the war, and was going to refuse until the fellow's wife said, "He really wants you to have it, because you saved his life." B.J. wears it now at all his concerts, and has gotten a lot of support from veterans, and dedicates "Raindrops" to this guy whenever he sings it.

Backstage, before we taped, B.J. and I were talking about how amazing it is that we reach the people we do in this business. He had done this song when he was a hippie, really, and never thought who might listen to it, or how it might affect someone on the other side of the world.

We also had some of the same vets I'd visited in the audience. We tried to find our escort officer, OB. I asked Johnny if he could help. We asked a lot of people, but had no luck finding him. Still, it was a really good show. There was a lot of reminiscing, we shared photos and stories, and Johnny brought along some of his home movies of the trip. One woman stood up and said, "You called me one night to tell me you had just seen my son, and I was so touched such a young girl would take time out of her busy life to do that, I started bawling." And so did I.

While still doing Carol's show, I became a regular on her 1970 summer replacement, *Carol Burnett Presents the Jimmie Rodgers Show*. This wasn't too long after his mysterious "accident," which he claimed had been an intentional attack on him. I don't believe the case was ever solved. I do know he wound up with a metal plate in his head. Jimmie was a very mellow guy and was able to joke about it. He used to say things like he couldn't go out in the sun anymore because his plate would get too hot.

There was lots of singing, lots of music, and lots of dancing on the show. Lyle Waggoner, Don Crichton, and I were the regulars from *Carol Burnett* to appear on Jimmie's show. Every week Don and I would do a big dance number, the reason I now refer to that season as "The Summer That Ruined My Knees." They are so embarrassingly noisy, I try never to walk up stairs with someone I don't know, and if I do, I talk really loud.

We did a wide variety of dance numbers. One week Roger Williams was the guest. We danced to his "Theme from Romeo and Juliet," which was a top ten hit at the time. Another week we did a Roaring Twenties tap number. We were like the "Bobby and Sissy" of summer replacements.

Jimmie liked to have his friends on as guests, one of whom was the Nashville singer/songwriter Bobby Russell. Bobby sang "Saturday Morning Confusion," a hit tune he'd written about a dad getting up with a hangover and the kids wanting to go out for breakfast.

Bobby's music is probably the thing that first attracted me to him. I confused the person with the songs. I thought, God, this is a really neat, sensitive guy. What I didn't know at the time was that Bobby wrote about a life he wished existed for him, one that was totally idyllic, but the furthest thing from reality.

People used to get Bobby Russell and Bobby Goldsboro confused, because Bobby Russell wrote "Honey" and Bobby Goldsboro had the hit with it, and between them they won something like ninety-four Grammys. Roger Miller recorded the country version of Bobby's "Little Green Apples" and was the best man at our wedding. Roger was a great guy, even if he was a little hyper, which was understandable since he used to keep uppers on him at all times and pop them like M&Ms. Whenever he'd lick his finger and reach in his pocket, you knew he was going for a pill.

During the week he was on the show, Bobby and I kind of hit it off, and would sit in the audience together for rehearsals and chat. He had that Southern genteel hospitality, which made him really easy to talk to. At one point he told me he was coming back to L.A. soon and asked if he could see me again. I said sure, and he added, almost in passing, that he had some problems at home he had to sort out. Being the idiot that I was, it never dawned on me the problems he was referring to were with a wife. I would never have gotten involved with him if I'd known he was married.

Before Bobby, I tended to go through guys rather quickly. If I felt it wasn't someone I wanted to spend the rest of my life with, I'd drop him just like that. I wasn't interested in having a relationship simply because it was a nice thing to do. I figured if it wasn't going anywhere, why waste my time? I'd rather sit home and read a book. The one thing I'm really proud of is that I wasn't promiscuous as a child. From the time I was a little girl my mother had convinced me that if I so much as French-kissed a boy I would get pregnant.

About the same time I started seeing Bobby, Harvey introduced me to McLean Stevenson and we went out a couple of times. McLean was a lot of fun. It didn't take long for me to know I was crazy about him, but I wanted to stay loyal to Bobby, and besides, McLean was a lot older than me. So, after two dates I said I couldn't see him again, because I was "seriously involved," but that I really liked him as a friend.

I'll take credit for convincing Mac to do the pilot for *M*A*S*H*. He was up for the part of Lieutenant Colonel Henry Blake when we dated. He said he didn't see how they could possibly turn that movie into a TV series. I thought he was wrong. I remember going over to the William Morris Agency to pick up the pilot script for him, reading it and telling him I thought it was going to be a wonderful series and he had to do it.

I asked him if he'd seen the movie and he said no. "Well, then, how do you know what you're talking about, you big goon," I said. "Let's go see it."

By this time—remember, this is before videos—the only place we could see the movie was in the old Rialto, a Spanish language movie theater in downtown L.A.

As we watched the film McLean and I were the only ones who laughed at the right time. Everyone else had to read the subtitles. We'd laugh, thirty seconds later they'd laugh; while they'd laugh we'd miss the next couple of lines, which would make us laugh even harder. We wound up laughing ourselves silly.

*B*obby started staying at my apartment every time he came to L. A. Finally, I decided it was about time he met my parents, and that's when it first became obvious to me (and them) that Bobby had a drinking problem. Because we were Christian Scientists, there was no drinking in our house, although every once in a while when we would go out for a birthday or something, mom would have a frozen daiquiri. She was raised Protestant. Still, the night I took Bobby to my parents' home proved a total disaster. He was so bombed he went to the bathroom to use the toilet and fell asleep on the bowl. It seemed like it took me forever to wake him up through the locked bathroom door with my parents sitting in the living room staring at me.

There was a lot of apologizing on my part and we were out of there.

Not long after, I'm not sure why or how, but I know it must have had something to do with meeting Bobby, I had one of the weirdest conversations with my mother. She came over to my apartment and frantically knocked on the door. I opened it and found her crying. She said she wanted to tell me about her sex life, which is not something I particularly wanted to hear. When I was younger I was sure she and dad had done it only twice, once for me and once for Joni. This day, though, she wanted to unload about how dad "hopped on and hopped off," and how it was horrible for her and what should she do, and I kept thinking, *I don't want to know this!*

I said, "Buy dad a Masters and Johnson book or something."

"He won't read it!"

"Well, I can't help you!"

Shortly before Bobby and I were married, I had to go to England to tape a Burnett show. I asked Bobby to come along and he said, "I ain't payin' to go all the way to Europe." So I downgraded my first-class ticket to coach and used the difference to cover his fare.

It was a very nice trip, except that I got the distinct feeling nobody on the show cared very much for Bobby. He was not what any of them would have described as a naturally "wonderful guy," on top of which he had that endearing Southern way of saying things that now seemed to me to be more offensive than charming. Worse, when he'd say something people would look at *me* in disbelief. Still, he came along and as long as we kept to ourselves we had a pretty good time.

When we got home, I had a free day before going back into rehearsals for the next week's show. That afternoon mom called and said she needed to see me right away. When I got to her house she told me that Bob Wright, the associate producer of the Burnett show, had called her earlier that day. "He's extremely upset."

"Why?"

"Well," she said, "everyone on the staff knows, and apparently it's spread through town, that you've been sleeping around Europe with someone you're not married to."

"My God!"

"And," she added, "I think they're going to fire you. You have to get down there right away."

I was petrified! Bobby and I had been with these people in England for two weeks, and because of it I was now about to be canned! I drove right down to CBS and went straight to Bob Wright's office. Yes, he said, he had called, and was happy that I could come right over.

He sat down behind his desk and gestured for me to take a seat as well. "Vicki," he said, and I felt my throat go dry, "I don't quite know how to say this." I felt my heart in my stomach. "We have to do something about your mother."

All the tension drained from my body as I realized in a moment of great relief I wasn't the problem. I was also incredibly embarrassed. "She's been driving everyone crazy," he said. "She calls the secretaries constantly while she feeds them weird stories and keeps them on the phone sometimes for hours. I don't know what we're going to do, but we have to find a way to get her to stop calling." I was so happy I wasn't fired and that nobody on the show gave a shit if I was sleeping all over Europe with Bobby, I practically threw my arms around Bob and promised him I would do everything in my power to control my mother.

I don't know why it took so many years to realize it was mom, not me, who was the weird one. Years later, when I was married to Al, he was doing the makeup for *All in the Family,* which taped on Sundays at CBS. One day Jean Stapleton came in a little bit late and Al was waiting for her in the makeup room. She looked at Al quite angrily and said, "Your mother-in-law is a nut case!" Jean happens to be a Christian Scientist too, and had run into my mother outside the church in Beverly Hills. "That woman stopped me on the steps to tell me what a hideous daughter she had and what a son of a bitch she married, and would not let me go. That woman is out of her mind!" This, from sweet, gentle Jean Stapleton! *Edith!*

Bobby and I were married in June 1971, just after the end of the Burnett show's fourth season. I don't remember much about my wedding day besides the fact that my sister and my parents didn't come to it. They were all devastated that I was actually marrying Bobby. I'm sure my mom insisted they not come as a way of demonstrating her anger. And nobody showed up from the show either.

*B*obby and I were living in a house in Benedict Canyon when I recorded "The Night the Lights Went Out in Georgia." On one of his trips to Nashville, Bobby had recorded demos of all his new material with a musician named Chip Young. When he was finished, I said, "What about 'Georgia'?"

"I hate that song," Bobby said.

I looked at him and said what I knew. "That song is a smash."

"If you like it so much, you demo it," he said, and left the studio for the nearest bar. So I did. Chip, who could play anything, laid down a piano track, then rolled the tape back, put the drums down, then rolled it back and added the bass, and finally, I sang the vocal to that track. When it was finished, Bobby took the demo to his producer in Hollywod, Snuff Garrett.

At the time Snuff had just signed a deal with Bell Records, and had intended to give my demo to Liza Minnelli. I said, "Liza Minnelli doing a country song? I don't get it."

He said, "You're right. I'll send it over to Cher." Unfortunately, she never got to hear it. Sonny rejected it for her because he felt it would tick off the half of the country that lived below the Mason-Dixon line. He strongly suggested Bobby rewrite it. Bobby refused, saying he "never liked the fucking song to begin with," and didn't want to waste another minute on it. So Snuff said, "Oh hell, let's just do it with Vicki." I lobbied hard for Artie Butler, a terrific arranger, to work on the song. I still think Artie was instrumental, if you will, in making it a hit. We laid down

98

the orchestra, I sang, overdubbed all the harmony parts, Snuff mixed it, mastered it, dubbed it, and had it in the tape box on the way to New York in only three hours. To this day he claims it as his record-holder. Whenever I hear it I say, "Gee, I wish I could have done that harmony part one more time."

It took nine months to become a hit, during which time I kept wondering when I was going to hear it on the radio. The big top forty station in Los Angeles at the time was KHJ-AM. One day I was driving home from work and "the real Don Steele" came on and said, "This next song is by Vicki Lawrence, and she is good!"

I was so excited I could hardly drive! I said to myself, "My God, I've arrived!" I pulled into the garage still on this incredible high, walked into the house, and discovered that one of the dogs had taken a dump on the living room carpet. So there I was, down on my hands and knees, cleaning up dog poop and crying all the time, telling myself, "I'm good, I'm good, I don't have to do this!" There's nothing like dogs and kids to keep you humble.

"The Night the Lights Went Out in Georgia" earned a gold record for me, and looking back, I think that was one of the major reasons my marriage failed so quickly. Bobby got really jealous of my new success, and we were quarreling horribly. He didn't want me to make any more

records, even as Snuff was threatening to sue if I didn't show up for our scheduled album recording dates.

I became so depressed at being caught in the middle, the album turned out hideously. There was one song from it that did fairly well behind "Georgia," called "He Did With Me," and I had one other go to number one in Australia, "Ships in the Night," but that was the effective end of my recording career. Still, the record's success added to my visibility. I had DJs calling to congratulate me and ask where I'd been.

I'd tell them, "Why, I've been on *The Carol Burnett Show* for five years."

It was as if I had appeared out of nowhere. And still, people could never figure out who I was. They could never put the whole thing together. Actually, I have a theory that people take Carol Burnett and Vicki Lawrence, mush the whole thing together, and come out with Carol Lawrence.

I used to do *Password* with Allen Ludden a lot. During the commercial breaks, the celebrity guests would take questions from the audience. One day a lady raised her hand, stood up and said, "I'd like to ask Carol Lawrence what it was like to be married to Robert Goulet?" Allen looked at me, hardly able to wait for my answer.

I said, "Well, he was a real son of a bitch and I divorced his ass!" The woman was in shock, but it got a great laugh from the crew. A few months later I ran into Carol Lawrence at a Christmas party in Hollywood and told her the story. She listened, nodded, and said, "That's the right answer, honey. Keep up the good work!"

On the heels of the song's success I got a commercial in New York. Now, I'm thinking to myself, everybody will finally know me. I got off the plane in New York and the girl from the ad agency was there to meet me. "Oh, Miss Carr," she said, smiling and excited, "we're so happy to have you here!"

For a brief period after "Georgia," Bobby and I formed a nightclub act and played Harrah's at Lake Tahoe together. We opened for Glen Campbell and the engagement was quite successful. After that, though, things between Bobby and me deteriorated even further.

His idea of a great home life was too much coffee, too many uppers, and too much booze. One time he got so angry he actually threw a wire hanger at me that hit me in the face. I don't remember what we were fighting about, but I do remember it really scared me. Bobby loved to fight. Not only did I hate it, I didn't know how. He would blow up over the slightest provocation, real or imagined. If he didn't like my cooking, he would pick up his dinner plate and throw it against the wall, or get drunk, turn on the stereo really loud and listen to it until three or four in the morning, while I went to bed and tried to sleep.

He also refused to pay for anything in our marriage because, he claimed, he was not a California resident. He insisted for tax purposes it was better if I paid for everything. He did give me the money for the deposit on our first home, a two-story colonial house in Beverly Hills, but I made all the payments after that. I also paid all the grocery bills, the gardener, the pool man, the insurance, the housekeeper, you name it.

Still, everything I did was wrong as far as he was concerned. If I was too good in bed, he'd say, "Who have you been practicing with?" I had no idea what he was talking about. I had nothing to measure our sex life against, as I'd never been with any other man before in my life.

Ironically, Bobby's mother was the sweetest person who ever lived. She loved to pinch my cheeks and say, "You are just the cutest little darlin' baby angel on this earth!" The first time I met her was the year Bobby and I were married, when he took me to his parents' home in Nashville for Christmas. I loved the thought of finally spending the holidays in the east. I couldn't wait to have a white Christmas, until Bobby said, "Don't get your hopes up. It hardly ever snows in Nashville."

Sure enough, in the middle of the night on Christmas Eve, it snowed. It was only a light dusting, but enough for me.

Bobby's mom was a typical Southern cook. She made the best deep-dish apple pie I've ever had, and fried everything else. She used to keep a tin of bacon grease in the kitchen window. Each time we'd visit I'd gain twelve pounds. Her fresh collard greens had bacon grease in them. Her cold-water hoe-cakes were soaked in bacon grease. Then there was her chicken-fried steak. At least there was no bacon grease in that.

Meanwhile, Bobby's dad would sit around watching *All My Children* and argue with the characters on TV. *"Damn it, what the hell do you think you're doing, going off with him . . ."* That Christmas I fell in love with Erica Kane and Duffy. Erica was a character on *All My Children*. Duffy was Bobby's dog. Duffy loved women. After we were married, whenever Bobby raised his voice to me, Duffy would get up on his hinders and growl at him. It was the cutest thing!

As I said before, Bobby was a voracious drinker. His favorite was gin martinis, and I didn't get the attraction. I did love those green olives, though. One time he took the pimento out and filled the pithole with a little gin and handed it to me. That was how I had the first alcoholic drink of my life.

Bobby and I were divorced less than a year after we got married, just about the time Mama made her first appearance on *The Carol Burnett Show*.

I based a lot of Mama on Bobby's mother, *"Little darlin' baby angel . . ."* although physically she looked like my mother's mother, Cora Loyd. Mama, like my grandmother, had a little gray perm from the beauty parlor and always wore a polyester frock. I'm sorry grandma didn't live to see Mama. I'm sure she would have gotten a huge kick out of her. Char, the psychic, insists that she *has* seen her, which is something of a comfort to me. I loved grandma.

Mother, of course, hated the character of Mama, was certain it was based on her, and resented me for it. One night, after seeing one particular sketch in which I played Mama on the show, she called me and we got into a big argument. She felt I played Mama too mean. At one point she said, "You take that lady way too seriously."

"*I* take her way too seriously?"

In 1972 Carol took the show on location to the grand opening of the Sydney, Australia, Opera House. I begged Bobby to go with me, but he refused. By this time our marriage was all but over, and anyway, he didn't like to travel very much. He also knew the people from the show weren't crazy about him, so he decided to stay home. Just before I left he called Al on the phone and said, "Take care of my old lady when you're in Australia. Keep an eye on her for me. I'll be in Nashville." Al said he'd be happy to. Meanwhile, he'd asked his wife to come, and she didn't want to go either.

Al and I had been good friends for a long time, one of the reasons Bobby thought he'd be the perfect chaperon for me. We used to double-date, Al and his wife, Bobby and me. Every time Al would have a fight with his wife, he'd come to our house. That's why it's so funny that after twenty years Al's ex-wife has resurfaced to tell the world how upset she is that I stole her husband.

When Reba McEntire was on my talk show, we commiserated about it because the same thing had happened to her. She said, "Well, I may have ended up with someone else's husband, but Vicki, you can't steal someone who ain't ready to leave!"

A lot of times Al would show up at our front door and spend the afternoon male bonding with Bobby. And when Bobby was gone, usually to Nashville, which was, looking back, where he spent most of the time we were married, Al would come over and bemoan the horrible marriage he was stuck in. It was like every ten minutes he was running away from home. He'd been married for six years, and they were separated more than they were together. I think it was one of those marriages that happen when men suddenly decide the time has come to settle down. It usually happens in their mid-twenties, often with an older woman. Al's wife, Sherry, was six years older than he was.

The first time I laid eyes on Al was in 1968. It was the first week of the show's second season, and I was sitting in Carol's dressing room at CBS, talking with her and Joe's secretary, Charlene. Al happened to walk by and my first impression was adorable, good-looking, tall, blond, and handsome. Plus, he was an ex–football player so he had a great tight end. He was dressed well right down to his skinny tie and what can I say, he caught all of our eyes. Carol was the one who spoke up first. "Who is that?" she asked, and Charlene said, "That's Al Schultz, the new makeup man in the building."

Carol said, "I don't care if he doesn't know what a powder puff is, I want him on my face tomorrow." I'm sure she meant that in a purely professional sense.

Charlene said, "Are you out of your mind? You've got the head of CBS makeup doing you now, you can't just bring in some kid you don't even know."

"He's adorable, get him," Carol said, and the next week he was doing her makeup. Two or three years later, he was the new head of CBS's makeup department, the youngest the network had ever had, and he quickly made his presence felt. He was the first to bring a black person into the makeup union, and the first to bring in a woman.

He became my makeup man on the show as well, and soon enough we became friends. At first I didn't speak to him at all, because my take on men at the time was that if they were gorgeous, they had to be snobby and would therefore not even spit on me. As a defense mechanism, I tended to act aloof around them. Al, as I gradually found out, like most big guys, was very gentle, and, to my delighted surprise, very sweet. Our friendship grew over the years and yes indeed, he certainly kept his eye on me in Australia.

My first two days down under I felt sick to my stomach. The hotel house doctor had to come up to my room and give me a shot. After, Al and I went to dinner a couple of times, and I started to feel real strange, and it had nothing to do with my stomach.

One night the whole gang from the show went out disco dancing. Edward Villella, the star of the New York City Ballet, was the show's special guest star that week, but now he was the star performer in the middle of the dance floor. Watching this male ballet dancer disco was an absolute delight. He was very sexy, very Italian, and, as all the girls soon found out, very horny. Al has often said that because of Edward Villella, in his next life he wants to come back as a straight ballet dancer. All the women wanted him. Everyone had a really good time and when we got back to the hotel, Villella offered to walk me to my room.

Al said, "Uh-uh. You're not walking her to her room. I am." On the way upstairs, he said to me, "He's not going to do any pirouettes on your navel."

Harvey was the first person to know that Al and I were in love. We went to dinner with him and his then wife, Donna, one night in Sydney, to a little Italian restaurant. Halfway through dinner Harvey looked at both of us and said, "You two assholes are in love with each other and too stupid to know it." He embarrassed the hell out of both of us.

The first night *I* knew I was in trouble was when Al and I went to dinner at a local fish restaurant. It was a bring-your-own-wine place right on the water. It was raining lightly, and when we crossed the street to catch a cab, Al put his arm around me. I couldn't help but notice it felt awfully comfortable there. Back at the hotel, he walked me to my door and seriously kissed me good night.

Things got even more serious when we moved inside, to my hotel room sofa. I had bought this darling little rabbit fur jacket in England and now refused to take it off. I knew if I did, I was going to be in deep trouble. The rabbit jacket stayed on and got one hell of a workout!

When we returned from Australia, neither of us felt any dwindling of feelings. It wasn't as if we "came to our senses," back in the real world. The unavoidable truth was that both of us had fallen head over heels in love, and knew it. We looked at each other and said, "This is ridiculous," we had always been such good friends. We'd never even used each other's first names; it was always, "Hey, Schultz," "Hey, Lawrence." And now, here we were!

We stopped in Hawaii on the return flight, where Al got off to meet his wife, who had gone there while we were in Australia and where, I don't think coincidentally, her ex-husband happened to be. I remember watching Al go through customs, then catching my flight to Nashville and crying all the way there because I was now so in love with him.

I arrived in Nashville only to discover my luggage was lost, which made Bobby furious. He blamed me for the missing bags, insisting somehow it was all my fault. Here I was, all the way from Australia, thirty-one hours of nearly nonstop flight time, emotionally exhausted, and I had Bobby screaming at me. I remember apologizing in some sort of fog, just wishing I could go home and lie down.

The night after I returned, he insisted on having a friend over to his farm. I vividly remember this because it was the first time I ever cussed at him. He was upset about dinner, I hadn't cooked it properly, and he was berating me about it. I got so fed up I turned and said, "Fuck you."

Bobby's reaction was to tell me he didn't want to see

me anymore, that we were officially separating, and insisted I return immediately to Los Angeles. I thought to myself, fine, I *want* to go home.

I got back to L.A. and spent the next couple of days moping around the house. Finally, I called Donna, Harvey's wife, who said, "You shouldn't be there all alone. Come on over and stay with us."

Incidentally, during the Australia trip Donna had had an affair with Edward Villella, and I was the only one who knew about it. She was running in and out of Villella's room every five minutes, just as happy as could be! I remember when I arrived at Donna's house that day there was this copy of *Life* magazine on the coffee table open to a full-page photo of Edward leaping in midair, wearing almost nothing, and looking gorgeous. The caption asked, "Is this the greatest athlete in the world?" According to Donna, the answer was a definite yes.

Anyway, I turned to Donna for help. At the time, Donna was having her own problems, not to mention two kids to raise and a house to run. She somehow managed to listen to me nonstop until one morning she announced, "You're going to a shrink today. You're driving yourself and me crazy. You need someone to listen."

So for the first time in my life, I went to see a psychiatrist.

Dr. Coodley's office was in Westwood, not very far from where Donna lived. Still, I managed to be late for my appointment. I jumped on the elevator, went to the wrong floor, got off, walked into the wrong office, and said, suddenly, "Oh my God, where am I?" I had to leave, get back on the elevator, go all the way back to the ground floor, catch another one, and go to the right floor. When I finally arrived at Dr. Coodley's office the first thing he said was, "You're late."

"I know. I'm sorry," I said. "I got off on the wrong floor, walked into the wrong office, and—"

"That was a deliberate avoidance, Vicki."

"No," I insisted. "I was on the elevator with a lot of other people, and just got off on the wrong floor!"

"No. You did it deliberately."

I thought about it and decided he was right. Fear of the unknown and all. We had a good talk, or should I say I did, and I decided to keep seeing him. He would lead me to a point where I would start talking about things, and in the middle of my sentence I would stop and say, "Oh my God, guess what!" when I understood the implications of what I was saying.

One day he said to me, "When did you move away from home?"

I explained to him why I got my apartment.

"But when did you really move away from home?"

"When I married Bobby?"

"You know, Vicki, I don't think you've moved yet."

"What are you saying, that Bobby and my mother are alike?"

"What do you think?"

What the psychiatrist was trying to show me was that I was sort of used to odd, abusive behavior, almost expected it, and probably sought it out. That's when I started thinking about all the verbal abuse I'd taken from the both of them, how they both insisted everything I ever did was wrong, that I was always apologizing, that it was always the same drill, just a different drill sergeant. "Same house, different room," was how Dr. Coodley put it.

I learned a lot about relationships, that they're a two-way street, and that people will stay in one as long as they're getting whatever it is they need from it. If it's abuse, if we don't feel good about ourselves, we'll stay in a bad relationship until we no longer require it. We all know where the exit door is. Going through it is the hard part.

Dr. Coodley was right. I hadn't left home at all.

One day he asked, "How would you feel about your

mom coming in? I really would like to talk to her."

I said, "I don't think she'll come."

"Why?"

"Because she thinks psychiatrists are for crazy people."

"Will you ask her?"

"I'll be happy to, but it won't do any good."

I left his office, went directly to her house, asked if she would see him and she said no, she didn't have the time because of her "illness." She was developing glaucoma, or so she claimed. Her doctor told her she would go blind if she didn't put these drops in her eyes every day. I said, "Mom, how long does it take to put in eyedrops? We can do the appointment any time of the day you want." The answer was still no. She still used the eyedrops as her excuse for not being able to go to see Dr. Coodley. I went back and told him she wouldn't come, and he said he didn't believe me! Not only that, but he didn't believe I had really asked her!

A week or two later I went in for an appointment, Dr. Coodley was sitting at his desk with his head in his hands. He looked up and said, "Guess who just called me?"

I took a deep breath. "Mom?"

He rolled his eyes. "That woman is nuts."

Now, during a previous visit, I had told Dr. Coodley about how whenever my mother called me, I found I couldn't get off the phone with her, that she could keep me on the phone no matter what. "Mom," I'd say, "I'm going to be late for work," or "Mom, I have an appointment," and it wouldn't register. She'd just go on and on.

Mom: "So on Tuesday, we were really . . ."

Me: "Mom, I have to go."

Mom: "Yes, but let me tell you about . . ."

Me: "Mom, I have to go."

It got to a point where I could put the phone down and come back every once in a while, say "Uh-huh" into the receiver and go about my business. Worked for me.

To all of this Dr. Coodley would only say, "You're a grown woman, Vicki. You simply say to your mother you have to go now and hang up the phone."

Now I sat back and smiled sarcastically. "So Dr. Coodley, what happened?"

"Frankly, I couldn't get off the phone," he said.

"Oh really? *You're an adult, Dr. Coodley. Why didn't you tell her you had a ten o'clock appointment and hang up?*"

"She wouldn't let me."

"THANK YOU VERY MUCH!"

We also discussed Al quite a bit. Dr. Coodley said that we all have a natural tendency to repeat our mistakes and he was concerned that when I left Bobby I would get into the same kind of relationship with Al. I told him I knew that wouldn't happen. When he asked me why I was so sure, I told him, "Because Al is my friend, and Bobby isn't."

I stopped seeing Dr. Coodley when we got to the point where he wanted to analyze why I liked gardenias better than roses, or why I liked Colgate better than Crest. I couldn't care less about any of that. I do feel, however, that he helped me get to the bottom of a lot of things during a very stressful period of my life and I am really grateful for that.

*L*ooking back, I'd have to say I was lucky to get out of my marriage as quickly and cleanly as I did. As awful as the experience turned out to be, and it was pretty awful, I'm still not sure it was a total mistake. I don't look at anything one does in life as a mistake. I see it all as part of the learning process. Some of us just go about learning in different ways than others. Bobby had become a crutch of sorts to help me make the formal break from my family.

One day, while Bobby was still back in Nashville, Al

showed up at my door to tell me that he was leaving his wife. He said, "Now I know what love is supposed to feel like." He told me he didn't want me to feel any pressure, but that it was real between us, and because of it he was ending his marriage.

That night was the first time Al and I made love. After, I asked him if he would please stay with me and he said no, because he was sure Bobby was returning to Los Angeles. I asked him how he knew and he said he just had a feeling. Sure enough, at six A.M. the next morning, Bobby pulled into the driveway, walked in the house, found the empty bottle of Mateus Al and I had shared and the two wine glasses I had forgotten to clean up, and it was over for good between Bobby and me. I got in my car and drove back to Donna's.

Ironically, when we used to double-date, Bobby would always say, "Al is a great guy. You should be married to a guy like him."

Now I was totally conflicted and confused and not at all prepared to begin divorce proceedings. We hadn't even been married one year. I kept thinking to myself, *How Hollywood!*

Not long after, I returned to the house one day at lunch. I needed to talk some things over with Bobby. I went upstairs to the bedroom, opened the door and there he was in our bed asleep with another woman! I started shaking! I couldn't believe I was in the middle of what felt like some cheap movie. I went back downstairs, as quietly as I could, called him on the second line of our telephone. The phone rang and rang, and I said to myself, *you drunken son of a bitch, wake up!* He finally did and I told him in no uncertain terms to get that woman out of my room!

I flew into a tirade when she came down. I screamed at her, then went upstairs, yanked my beautiful antique quilt off the bed, stormed out, got halfway back to work before

I realized I wasn't going to be able to return to the show in my emotional state. I called Joe Hamilton and told him I needed a day off, that I was too upset, and he was very sweet about it. He told me I should take all the time I needed to get myself together, and hung up.

Then one evening, I went back to the house again, this time to get the rest of my things. Bobby was now living there with the woman and her child. When I arrived, I went to the coat closet where I kept my albums, and hanging right in front were two Nazi uniforms, complete with medals on the jackets. I looked at them, closed the door, and got the hell out of there, leaving everything.

I always knew Bobby was strange, but I never knew how much until I saw those uniforms. When we were married, he used to love to read about Göring, Goebbels, Hitler, the whole gang, which I wrote off at the time as intellectual curiosity. He once remarked that because I was part Jewish, if Hitler were still alive I'd surely be dead. I remember thinking at the time, thank you so much for sharing that lovely thought with me, Bobby!

Al invited me to move in with him. He had taken an apartment in West Hollywood. As much as I wanted to, I felt I had to say no, as I was still technically married to Bobby. So instead I rented my own apartment and don't believe I ever spent a single night there. I wound up going over to Al's place every night. Finally one day he said it was ridiculous for me to be spending money on an empty apartment when in reality we were living together at his place.

Meanwhile, Bobby was still living in our house. He insisted I sign a quitclaim deed or it would be an ugly divorce. I said fine. All I wanted out of the marriage was Duffy, the dog. One day, Bobby left me a message, saying that Duffy was going to cost me fifty thousand dollars. Otherwise he was going to take me to court and rake my ass over the coals and I'd never see that dog again.

That Friday night, after taping the show, I went out to dinner with Al. "Will you do me a favor?" he asked. "Go to the pay phone, call Bobby and tell him you don't give a shit about Duffy."

I told Al through my tears I just couldn't do that.

"It's a game, Vicki," Al said. "That's all he's got. If you tell him you don't want Duff, you'll get him. Call his bluff."

So I pulled myself together, called Bobby and told him I didn't care about Duffy, that I didn't want him anymore. "You heartless, cold bitch," he said. "You don't give a shit about anything or anybody, do you."

"No. Nothing and nobody," I said and hung up. It was the hardest thing I ever had to do. I adored that dog. And I'd often seen Bobby abuse him so badly, things like drop-kicking him when he was angry, probably the reason Duffy hated men so much.

We'd had another dog as well, Benji, a basenji. Bobby would get into really hideous bouts with Benji, who was a real fighter, while Duffy and I would hide in the bedroom and cower with fright.

Anyway, that night, after we got back to Al's apartment, there was a message on his phone machine from Bobby. "Come and get your fucking dog tomorrow, and don't you dare touch anything else."

The next day I went up to the house. No one was home. I found the two dogs in the service porch, where it looked as if they'd been locked up for days. It was nothing but wall-to-wall throw-up, runs, about the ugliest, most repulsive thing I'd ever seen. I cleaned up Duffy as best I could, just to be able to put him in my car. Benji wanted to come with us so badly, but I'd promised to take only Duffy. It broke my heart to look in his eyes and know I had to leave him behind.

Although Duffy mistrusted men, he and Al became fast friends. The only thing Al would do that Duffy didn't like was to lock him out of the room when we were making love, because Duffy would still growl and show his teeth whenever a man came near me.

Duffy had a really nice, long life. On Christmas Eve, 1976, he was really dragging. He looked like he was on his last legs. I went out to the patio, sat there and rocked him in my arms as I cried and talked to him about everything that we'd been through together, how much I loved him, and thought to myself, what a lousy night to lose Duffy.

Al saw how upset I was and said, "You know what, he probably just needs a little Christmas cheer." Al took the turkey baster, filled it with brandy, put it down Duff's throat, giving him a good shot, and assured me he'd be all right.

I went to the back door Christmas morning and sure enough ol' Duff was rarin' to go, barking, happy, rubbing his paws together. *"All right, it's Christmas, everybody, let's party!"*

He lived another four years. Al was the one who finally had to take him to be put to sleep. After all I'd been through with that dog, I just couldn't deal with it. Al took him to the vet, stayed with him until the end, then drove around for two hours crying like a baby.

For the longest time after we separated, Bobby kept trying to screw with my head. He'd call and tell me how really messed up I was, and that I didn't know what I was doing with my life. Al would come in and say, "Get off the phone, Vicki. Don't let him do this to you. Grow up!" It was Al who finally gave me the courage to permanently hang up on Bobby.

I went to the only attorney I knew, the one who had represented the Burnett show when I'd first joined it. His name was George Towers and I literally ran into him on the street one day in Beverly Hills. He was a really nice guy, and rightly suggested I consult a divorce lawyer. However, I didn't want to get any further entangled in Bobby's increasingly weird world. "Just get me out," I pleaded. So, in order to terminate things, I agreed to take nothing. Not that I wouldn't have loved to have kept that home in Beverly Hills, mind you. Al came out of his divorce the same way, with nothing more than the clothes on his back.

Because of the quitclaim I'd signed, Bobby got the house. He also kept the farm in Nashville, a herd of champion Charolais cattle he had given me that we had intended to breed, a palomino quarter horse and a thoroughbred that he'd given me, all my antiques, everything. At one point during the divorce proceedings he said to me, "All right, if you want your goddamn cattle, and your goddamn horse, I'm going to drive them out here and park them in front of your apartment," and I went oh no! *Like that could happen, Vicki.*

*A*l and I began living together in 1974, with combined assets totaling about $12,000. As far as we were concerned, that was okay, we could live quite nicely on love alone, which was lucky for us because that's about all we had. While we were waiting for our divorces to become final, we took every last dime we had and plunked it down on a darling little house in Sherman Oaks. I guess we just assumed we were going to be together forever.

Al's ex-wife found out where we were living, and decided to personally deliver all his mail. Not that there was a whole lot still going to his old address. She would separate occupant and resident letters. She was "resident," he was "occupant." She'd scream and yell and bang on the front door, wave something in the air and say, "I have a letter here *for my husband! You're sleeping with my hus-*

band, you slut!" I thought for sure that Duffy was going to go through this pretty antique beveled glass door we had and kill her!

One day we were backing out of the garage and she came driving along and tailgated us down Ventura Boulevard until Al managed to lose her. Then there was the time Rona Barrett received a "hot tip." I'm sure it came from Sherry. "What actress," Rona asked over the air, "who looks like Carol Burnett is driving around in a big expensive car that belongs to her boyfriend's ex-wife?"

We both heard it at the same time and Al said, "What is she talking about? I paid for that car!"

I was still working on the Burnett show and Al was by now the head of CBS's makeup department. One day Al came to me and wanted to know how I would feel about his leaving the network to freelance. It was fine with me, I told him. He said he'd gotten a really good offer to go work on *The Planet of the Apes* TV series. The pay was better than what he was earning at CBS, and he felt he could learn a lot as well. I encouraged him to go for it.

He looked at me and said that his first wife would never have allowed him to make such a move. I told him I couldn't understand that. If that's what he wanted to do, then he should do it. It's one of the things I've always loved about our relationship, how we've always been supportive of each other. Al once told me that I was the only one in his life who allowed him to be himself. I feel pretty much the same. We just try not to get in each other's way. As a result, we wind up being really good for each other.

*M*y favorite Christmas with Al has to be 1973—the first one we spent together. Al had just gone to court and told the judge that all he wanted were his personal things from the house. The judge made a ruling that on

Saturday he could go to the house and get his belongings.

That morning he showed up with a pickup truck, and sure enough, his about-to-be ex-wife had parked her car in front of the garage so that Al couldn't open the door. She and her mother and her first husband, whom she'd gotten back together with, were waiting for him, and started screaming that he wasn't going to come in the house. Al went in anyway and started gathering his things, and his wife called the police.

The police came with guns drawn, even as the ex-husband was helping Al load up the truck! The two women were standing, screaming in the doorway, while Al showed them the court order to prove that everything he was doing was legally sanctioned. One of the cops went inside to talk to the women, came back out and said to Al, "Why don't you just get out of here? There's no stuff on earth that's worth this. By the way," he asked, "who's this?"

Al said, "This is her first husband." The cop hit his head with his hand and said, "Sheesh!"

Al finished loading what he had already gotten out of the house and left. Unfortunately, he never got all of his things, many of which were irreplaceable, like the autographed John Wayne photo and rifle the Duke had personally given him.

It was several days before Christmas. Al had borrowed a cabin from the lady who did the hair on Carol's show, a little one-bedroom with no TV, a big stone fireplace, and a nice kitchen, out in the middle of the Lake Arrowhead woods, with snow on the ground, and squirrels coming to the back door every morning for their breakfast treats.

We bought each other one present, I don't even remember what they were, went for long walks, and Al did most of the cooking. We stayed there for three nights. The whole trip was so quiet and so romantic. I am living proof that doing it on a bearskin rug in front of a huge fire is everything it is cracked up to be!

• • •

One day in June 1974, shortly after both our divorces became finalized, we went to the Santa Monica antiques show and passed this vintage jewelry counter. I love antique anything, but especially jewelry. I put on a twenties cocktail ring with diamonds and garnets. It fit perfectly. The salesperson said it was fifteen hundred dollars. Al said he had only five hundred in the bank and the fellow said "Sold!"

"Well," I said, "this will make a really nice engagement ring, Al."

He said, "Oh, great, okay, I get the picture." I guess I proposed to him, and that was it. By the way, when I showed what I thought was this beautiful ring that I really loved to mom and asked her if she liked it, she shrugged her shoulders and said, "I guess if you like it, it's fine."

One morning that August I sat up in bed and said, "You know what, I haven't had a period in three months."

Al said, "Well, Vicki, don't you think you should check something?"

"Do you think maybe . . ."

"Yes I think maybe."

Now, you have to remember, my mom raised me so that I didn't know diddly-squat about *nothing from nothing*. So I went to Carol and asked if she had a good gynecologist. Up to that point I'd never even been to one. Carol gave me the name of hers. I made an appointment, had a pregnancy test, the doctor called the next day to tell me I was pregnant.

Even though we weren't married yet, we were so much in love it was quite exciting for us. Al had taken the job on *Planet of the Apes* and was working hideous hours. He'd have to get up at three in the morning, hit the road by four so he could be at Palos Verdes, where they would start shooting by five, do three hours of monkey makeup, shoot all day, get home by eight o'clock at night, maybe have a glass of wine and a bite to eat before passing out. He was working his butt off. He was in the lab working on rubber masks for *Planet,* and it was about 120 degrees in there. He picked up the phone and I said, "Hi, daddy." He says it was the most incredible feeling he'd ever had.

I didn't speak to my mother very much at all during the entire time Bobby and I were married. Now, I couldn't wait to tell her I was pregnant. When I did, she became hysterical. You'd have thought I had slept with the devil. I could never figure out her reactions.

*A*l and I planned a lovely wedding. He wanted to get married on a yacht, so he chartered an Alaskan 44. I had the invitations and everything done, and then one morning, three or four weeks before our wedding date, I got a call at the Burnett show, saying that Al had just fallen on the set of *Planet* and was in the hospital.

I rushed straight to Daniel Freeman Hospital. They had Al in bed with his leg hung up in a sling. While he bitched and moaned, the orthopedist took me aside. "This man is going to be dead before you ever give birth if you don't tell him to shut up and be a good patient. He's got phlebitis and if he's not careful, the clot will leave his leg and go straight to his heart." This was just around the time Nixon had phlebitis and it had become a very fashionable ailment.

Al, on the other hand, was saying, "Bullshit, you have to break me out of here." I found myself stuck between Al and the doctor, thinking, I just want to get married. Finally, Al said to me, "Look, I had this same injury when I was in college. Believe me, Vicki, I know what I'm talking about."

They had him on so many blood thinners he was out of

it, and still I found myself helping him break out of the hospital. As he was getting up, the nurses kept saying, you can't do this, you can't do this.

We got home, and the first thing Al did was to stop taking the blood thinners. He's probably lucky he didn't kill himself. He got a spiking fever, and I covered him with every blanket we had in the house. Each time it broke, everything on the bed would be soaked. He lost twenty-five pounds. I called the doctor to see what we should do, and the doctor said, and I think I'm quoting verbatim here, "I hope he dies. He's the worst patient I ever had."

I called my own doctor to find out how anyone could say such a thing. I said I wanted to sue that son of a bitch, and he said, "I'll tell you what. You're pregnant, you have a wedding coming up, you don't need to get mixed up in a lawsuit, and besides, you won't find a doctor to testify against another. Why don't you bring Al to see me instead."

My doctor, Bob Woods, was a really good GP who happened to be the doctor for the Los Angeles Dodgers. I felt that was a plus for us, because Al is an ex-jock. So I bundled him up and drove him to St. John's Hospital, where Al was assigned to Dr. Watanabe, the UCLA sports specialist. He checked Al in and the lab technicians asked if we had any X-rays. Well, we didn't, because the other doctor had never ordered any!

They took him immediately down to X-ray, and the guy in the basement in the lab took one look and said, "This isn't phlebitis. I see this all the time with the football players. He's just torn his calf muscle and the leg's filled up with blood. You need to drain it before he loses his leg."

That's exactly what we did. Dr. Watanabe went to Al's room with a huge hypodermic needle, punched a hole in Al's calf, and drained about six ounces' worth of really black blood. A day or so later Al was discharged and I took him home.

I remember grabbing Al in bed one night soon after and screaming at him, "YOU BETTER MARRY ME NOW, YOU SON OF A BITCH! I DON'T WANT MY CHILD TO BE A YEAR OLD BEFORE WE TIE THE KNOT!"

We canceled the boat, and held a little wedding at the house in Sherman Oaks. Al had a lot of codeine in him, washed down with champagne. As a result, we didn't have much of a wedding night, but he did look very sexy in the photos!

The best wedding gift we received was from Carol and Joe—two round-trip tickets to our favorite place in the world, Maui. When we got to Hawaii, they took Al off the plane in a wheelchair. After two weeks of warm sand and tropical water, he walked back on the plane with just a crutch.

It was around this time Al and I sat down and compared paychecks. Al may have thought he was getting himself a wealthy woman, but in reality, he was clearing more than I was. People don't realize that actresses pay ten percent to an agent, five percent to a business manager, a fee to a publicist, and by the time you get through with Uncle Sam, a lot is gone.

As Al continued to recuperate, I turned to him one night and asked, "Do you think someone is trying to tell us something?"

"What do you mean," he asked.

"You've been working astronomically hideous hours, I'm working, we don't get to see each other that much, and the simple fact is I have the capacity to make more money than you." So we made a pact that he would leave makeup and I would get rid of all the other people in my business life (some of whom, by the way, had screwed me over pretty badly). Al would take charge and we would try to hang on to what I made. In the long run it's been great for the kids, because it's meant that almost always one of us has been there for them.

Perhaps not surprisingly, it took Al a while to get used to mom. I'd come home. Al would have the phone to his ear, saying nothing. After staring at him for the longest time, I'd say, "Who are you talking to?"

He'd hold the phone out to me, and I'd hear the familiar sound of my mother's voice rattling on and on. "Just say 'uh-huh' every once in a while. She'll never know the difference."

Like I told Dr. Coodley. *Works for me.*

Very pregnant and singing the "Lullabye Medley" on the
last show of the 1974–75 season.

The Moon Never Beams Without Bringing Me Dreams

It wasn't until my second season on *The Carol
Burnett Show,* in 1968, that I finally landed my first part
other than "Carol and Sis." I began doing "characters" and
appearing in many of the show's trademark musical fi-
nales. My favorites were the takeoffs of old movies with
big musical pieces like "The Funn Family," which we did
one year with John Davidson, Mickey Rooney, Carol, and
me. It was a takeoff on old vaudeville, with Harvey playing a character called Ziggy Flofeld! I also recall a terrific
takeoff we did on the 1945 film *The Dolly Sisters,* which
became the "Doily Sisters."

We did one on the classic Marlene Dietrich movie *The*

Blue Angel. Carol was Dietrich and Harvey was the German teacher. He was supposed to change out of his tuxedo and into a chicken suit, with head, feathers, and funny little feet. He was backstage making this quick change when Willie, our stage manager, pointed to him and said, "Cue, you're on!" The only problem was, Harvey hadn't gotten into the lower half of his costume yet.

"I'm not dressed, goddamn it," he said.

Willie pointed and said, "You! Get out there."

So Harvey did, in his chicken head, little feathers, and jockey shorts, and started singing. The audience went wild, Carol started laughing and before you knew it, we had to stop taping because she announced that she had just peed in her pants! Joel Grey, who was a "serious" stage actor, stood there with his mouth hanging open, not believing what he was seeing!

Harvey's dressing room had a long bathroom, shower, huge makeup room, and a lounge area. Carol had a huge place as well, but because Al only visited her when she needed makeup he set himself up in Harvey's room. Harvey used to take a Librium before the tapings.

When I asked him why, he said, "Oh God, I couldn't do the show without it!"

Harvey and Al were like the odd couple and liked to play practical jokes on each other. One night Al put peanuts in Harvey's Librium bottle, because Harvey would literally pick it up, take the cap off, and shake one into his mouth. When he realized they were peanuts, he started laughing and screamed, "Schultz, you asshole!"

I never knew it until one night I saw him taking two just before he went on. I said, "What are you doing?"

He said, "Laurence Olivier is in the audience."

"So? He's just a person, Harvey."

"You are so stupid," he shouted at me. "You probably don't even know who Laurence Olivier is!"

One year at the season wrap party, Harvey gave Al the

Up-Your-Acetone award. Al used to go through a lot of it with Harvey. It's awful-smelling stuff used to remove makeup prosthetics. Because Harvey sweat so much it was difficult for him to keep mustaches and toupees on without a ton of glue. This happened so often it became a running gag between the two. Harvey's mustache or sideburns would start to curl up under the hot lights, and Al would say to him, "Jesus, do you think you could have had a little more vodka last night?"

Without question, my most embarrassing moment on the show happened when Hal Linden was on, and we did a takeoff of *Show Boat*. I was the Jeanette MacDonald–type ingenue and he was Howard Keel. We were supposed to do a send-up of the song "We Could Make Believe." Our version was called "Pretend." Carol has always claimed that I have perfect pitch, which isn't quite true. I do have a pretty good ear, though, and can come close on any given day, if I'm lucky.

Anyway, I was standing face-to-face with Hal, who is a trained stage actor and excellent singer, and I was supposed to start the song. There was an arpeggio on the piano, after which I was to sing, *Pretend . . . pretend . . .* Now, in rehearsals, the arpeggio ended on my starting note. For some reason, the night of the show, it was totally different. I hit the first note and it was in the stratosphere. I sounded like a fire engine siren! And then it came again, and again I was all the way up there! Hal just glared at me.

Carol came out of her dressing room, stood on the side of the stage, saw what was happening and howled! I looked at Hal, who was still glaring, and said, "Well, you're a lot of help," and went into a series of exploratory *pretends . . .* Finally, the piano player went ding, ding, ding, on my starting note. God, it was awful.

Needless to say, the sketch didn't air that way.

It wasn't until five years after I'd joined the show, when

Mama happened, that I finally felt I was carrying my full weight. Until then, it was like I was in school, albeit state-of-the-art hands-on training at the best comedy school in the world.

Still, at times, it seemed as if Joe Hamilton wanted to control every aspect of my personal as well as professional life. One time I went and got my hair permed and styled into a "natural." It was the in thing to do back then. Joe called me into the office one day and said, "We're getting a lot of fan mail from people who think you're half black."

"What? They think I'm black?" Me, the all-American slice of white bread come to life? I couldn't understand why all of a sudden I was being criticized for such mundane things. However, that incident paled, no pun intended, when that same year I became pregnant with Courtney and suddenly noticed that everybody at work had stopped speaking to me.

I'd go home at night crying, so depressed, until Al finally asked, "What is it, honey?" I told him I didn't know why, but no one was talking to me at work. I'd go in and do my lines and feel ostracized. Al picked up the phone to Joe and asked him just what the hell was going on.

"Well, there's a little thing in her contract called the 'deformity clause,' " Joe said. "Listed under it are things like broken legs, scars, facial changes, and pregnancy." Lovely, I thought to myself. According to my contract, pregnancy was a deformity!

Joe said he was going to lay me off for the last eight weeks of the season. Al said, "You're going to lay her off, not even pay her, not even speak to her, like she's got some kind of terrible disease just because she's pregnant?"

Joe thought about it, and I guess he felt bad, because he called back a week later and offered to give me half pay, but refused to budge about taking me off the show.

I finally got the nerve to talk to him myself and he said, "Look, the feeling around here, very frankly, is that you should be sitting at home with your feet up in the air knitting booties." I thought to myself, I'm dealing with the biggest male chauvinist pig who ever lived!

"Correct me if I'm wrong," I said to him, "but Lucy had her kids during a commercial break!"

He said, "That was her show."

I said, "Okay, fine. Cher is next door taping a show with her ex-husband, and she's pregnant with another guy's child."

"Yes," he said, "but that's Cher and that's her image, not Carol's."

"It's not Carol's image that women have children? Carol had every one of her kids by immaculate conception?"

End of discussion. I was still laid off.

Three weeks later Carol decided she couldn't stand not doing Eunice so they wrote a sketch where Mama had sprained her ankle. Whenever I see it in reruns it cracks me up because I'm in this wheelchair with so many blankets on me I look . . . *pregnant!*

When I came out at the end of that show for the goodnight I wore one of my own maternity dresses and the entire country then saw that I was indeed "with child." I finished the rest of the season as if the whole pregnancy incident had never happened. I suspect what really happened was that when Joe laid me off, Carol said, "That's bullshit," and brought me back.

It wasn't until the end of the final show of the season that Carol announced I was indeed expecting—after all, I was out to here by then and looked like Jaba the Hut! We did a beautiful medley of lullabies, and Courtney was on the first show of the next season, so that everyone could see how I spent my summer vacation!

• • •

So, as I mentioned earlier, Bob Mackie was in charge of costumes for *The Carol Burnett Show*. Bob, God love him, was very intense about his work. He's mellowed a lot over the years, but in those days he used to regularly fly off in rages. He came on *Vicki!* with Carol one time and said during the show's run he had forty-five seamstresses who did nothing but work on our costumes.

He usually produced something like sixty to eighty costumes a week. We used to laugh and make jokes about him, how he must have had a ruler to beat the knuckles of the women putting on the little bugle beads for Carol's gowns.

If any of the regular cast wasn't in the show's finale that week, they were supposed to come out in black tie for the final good-nights. I had a special black dress that Bob had designed for me to use for such occasions.

I was never thin enough to suit Bob. Cher was his idea of weight perfection. I had spent the entire summer losing the sixty-four pounds I had put on during my pregnancy. As a reward, he decided to make a new good-night outfit for me. I was so flattered!

I always had my wardrobe fittings before Wednesday's rehearsal, and that was when Bob showed me my new outfit, a beautiful long skirt with a slit up to my thigh and a chiffon top. I put it on and you could see right through to what looked like two fried eggs under a sheer black thing. We had a good laugh.

He said, "Now, what I'm going to do here, so you'll know, is line the front half only, so that the back is still sheer. You won't need a bra with it." I said fine.

Tape day came. We never rehearsed the good-nights. When the time came, my dresser whipped out my new outfit. I put it on and there staring back at me in the mirror were my fried eggs! Cute, yes, but clearly inappropriate for *The Carol Burnett Show.* "I can't wear this," I said to my dresser. "You'll have to go downstairs and get my old dress."

By now, Willie, the stage manager, was at the foot of my dressing room stairs yelling, "Vicki, let's go, we're waiting for *you!*"

Carol's dresser came running up the stairs, while Carol and the rest of the cast were waiting for me. "What's the problem?"

I turned to her, dropped my hands and said, "*This* is the problem."

She took one look and said, "Just get out there."

Yeah, sure. I flashed on Carol singing, *"We're so glad we had this time together* . . . NICE TITS, VICKI! . . . *Just to have a laugh or sing a song . . ."*

When someone finally found Bob, he was absolutely livid. He had gone and gotten my old outfit himself, threw it at me, and said, "Here's your fucking dress!"

*H*arvey never liked doing the "Family" sketches. He thought all the characters were one-dimensional. He hated his character, Ed Higgins. He used to say "The only character worth a damn in the whole mess is Mama." Although many people still think so, Mama didn't appear on every show. It actually took the writers about five weeks to complete one Mama sketch. And when they did, it would sometimes run as long as twenty minutes, a full third of the show, very much like the original "Honeymooners" skits on Jackie Gleason's fifties variety show.

We had a lot of fun doing those "Family" sketches. Of course, there's Dick Clark's favorite outtake, which has become his all-time great blooper. It happened the last season of the show, after Harvey had left and Dick Van Dyke became a regular. Dick was playing a character who was supposed to be the love interest for Eunice. Tim Conway was still playing Mickey Hart like a goon, and Mama and Eunice and Mickey and Dick's character were playing Password on the sofa. The password was "silly."

The guys had the password, meaning, if you remember how the game worked, they were "giving." Mickey's clue to Eunice was "elephant." After they lost, and Eunice saw the word, she said to Mickey, "What the hell does 'elephant' have to do with 'silly,' you dumb cluck?" Tim, who never liked to rehearse, then launched into this story about an elephant he once saw in the circus. Carol rolled her eyes and smiled. "Actually there were two of them," he continued, "and they were Siamese elephants, joined at the trunk, and I felt really sorry for them, because they couldn't blow out of their trunks like other elephants, they'd blow their brains out." Carol put her head in her hands and groaned.

She was supposed to hand me the next password and say, "Okay, it's your turn, Mama," but by now she had tears in her eyes, from trying not to laugh. "Mama," she pleaded, her lips quivering. I stared at her disgustedly, like Mama would, for the longest time, until she broke down completely. Tim went, then we all went, and the sketch was an absolute disaster in front of the dress rehearsal audience.

Carol hated it when the "Family" sketches got screwed up. She never liked breaking the so-called fourth wall. But, whenever Tim was in them, forget it.

Between shows, Dave Powers, the director, would always come into our dressing room and give us our notes, things like, you missed your mark on the dance number, could you please do this sooner, we're making a cut here. That night Dave knocked on my door and said, "I only have one note. Tim's story's going to be different. Good luck."

Al happened to be in my dressing room. I turned to him and said, "How come Tim gets away with this shit all the time and nobody ever gets back at him? That really pisses me off."

Al said, "Well, get back at him."

"Okay, I'm going to." I didn't usually do that kind of thing, but this time I was determined. The second taping started, and the story had indeed been embellished. It was still about the Siamese elephants, but now they had a little trained monkey who came out to dance the merengue on their trunks. And again it just went on and on and on, and again Carol went, while I sat there telling myself Tim wasn't going to get me. Finally, Carol managed to get her line out. "Okay, Mama, it's your turn . . ."

I just stared at her, which made her laugh even harder, and then I said, "You sure that little asshole's finished?"

Well, both Tim and Dick went off the sofa like bookends. The audience went wild, even the cameras started shaking!

Of course, CBS bleeped the word "asshole," and a couple of days later my mother called to find out what I'd said. I told her, "Are you sure that little asshole's finished," and she said, "No you didn't."

"I know what I said, mom. I was there."

"You didn't say that."

"Yeah, I did."

"*No. You didn't.*"

In 1976, we did a show where I was really heavily featured. At one point Carol turned to me and said, "This is your Emmy show." According to academy rules, a show's executive producers, in this case Joe and Carol, were responsible for submitting names for nomination consideration. I had previously been nominated five times and was under the impression that the award was based on a performer's overall body of work on a series. In fact, it is based on one episode, like the one in which I was featured. On it I played a bimbo receptionist in the "B" sketch where just about every word began with the letter "B." It was set in a business office and I'd answer the phone by saying, "Burke, Burns, Brotton and Brokaw. How may I help you? Ball bearings? Please hold." I was also in the Mama sketch, and the big production number at the end.

As it happened, *Saturday Night Live* swept everything that year. Chevy Chase won in the male category. I was up against all the girls from the show, Gilda Radner, Laraine Newman, and Jane Curtin, and it looked as if they were going to win in a walk. When they announced the names of the nominees, Harvey took my hand and said, "Get ready to win your first Emmy, baby."

AND HE WAS RIGHT!

I couldn't believe it! I went up to the podium, and the Captain and Tennille handed me my Emmy. I said, "A lot of people think I'm in Carol's shadow. Well, I can't think of a nicer shadow to be in."

And I still feel that way.

Why Satellite TV Scares 102 Nations

TV GUIDE

15¢ Local Programs
March 16-22

·AMSEL·

Carol Burnett and Vicki Lawrence

Shortly after we were married, my dad sent Al a bill for twenty-five thousand dollars, what he figured it cost to raise me. Because he was an accountant, he had broken it down to the last dollar. Al and I went out to dinner that night, got drunk on gin martinis and had a huge argument about who had the worse family. When we got home, Al picked up the phone, called both our families and told them each to get lost. Al's mother immediately apologized, I'm not sure what for, but she wanted to be close to her granddaughter. My mother and dad wouldn't deal with that phone call for years.

We were now living in Benedict Canyon, and decided to have a big Thanksgiving dinner. Al's folks were invited along with a number of "orphans" from the show.

It was the first time I had ever actually made a whole turkey dinner from scratch, because my mother hadn't taught me how to cook. I didn't know a spatula from a colander. So I went down to the fanciest place I could find, Williams Sonoma, which had just opened in Beverly Hills. I walked in and said, "I need help." A friendly salesperson sold me a roasting pan, and what is to this day one of my favorite cookbooks, *How to Beat Those Cordon Bleus.*

I have had more people ask me for recipes out of that book than anything else. It tells every single step, so there's no way you can really screw anything up. It tells you how to serve, what you can prepare ahead of time, what you can freeze, what you can refrigerate, what wine to serve, everything. The one thing it did not tell me about the turkey was to take the giblets out. Who knew?

Now, Al's favorite thing is the giblets. The only problem that night was, I couldn't find them until we carved the turkey and out they came in their little douchebag. Worse, it happened in front of my mother-in-law.

It wasn't until 1980 that we patched things up with my parents to the point where we could have them over for Thanksgiving dinner. It also happened that my grand-mother was visiting and I really wanted to see her.

At one point, my mother decided she was going to help me in the kitchen. It's become a tradition in our house that Al always makes the gravy. He uses very little flour and skims off all the fat. However, that night, Mom in-sisted that she make the gravy, and wouldn't back down. Finally, Al let her have her way. When she finished, it was so thick it wouldn't come off the spoon. He then an-nounced that he was throwing it away and making his own. "If you want to make quadruple bypass gravy for your husband," he told her, "you can do that at your own house, on your own time. In my house, I make the gravy, and that's it."

Well, mom stormed out of the kitchen. My grand-mother, who was helping me serve, said softly, "I don't know where I went wrong . . ."

I said, "You did okay, grandma. You did fine."

Mom sat sulking in the living room during dinner, refus-ing to eat with anyone. The kids kept asking where she was. I finally had to go to her and say, "Are you going to be civil?"

She came back in, took a plate, helped herself to one dollop of creamed spinach, and never even touched that. She just stared at that plate for the entire dinner. When we were all done she asked, "Is everybody through? Good. Howard, let's go home." She then got up, took my father and left.

I had kind of given up on the whole religion deal early on, as had Al, who was born Lutheran. It's not that I don't believe in God, I do. I'm just not sure you have to go to church to be religious. So, when Courtney was born, Mary, Al's mother, asked me when the baptism was going to be, and I had to tell her as gently as possible there wasn't going to be any.

"What do you mean?" she said. "Your children will go to hell."

I then broke the happy news to her that I had never been baptized either. I tried to explain to her that Christian Scientists didn't believe in actually putting their head in water and that I considered baptism more a state of mind than a dip in the pool. She went absolutely nuts. I suggested to Al that for the sake of the kids, God, and his mother, not necessarily in that order, we all get baptized Lutheran. That way we'd at least be something.

And so we did.

When Al and I first got married we made a pact, promising each other to work very hard to keep all the outside forces, including family, friends, and co-workers, from destroying our marriage. As a result, we became very private, mostly to avoid all the unnecessary confrontations, and to not hear all of the garbage that people are always saying. It takes a very strong man to be able to handle Al's role in a marriage like ours.

Besides all the grief from our families, from the beginning of our relationship we were subjected to the kind of thing that still goes on in show business every day. When Dr. Joyce Brothers did *Vicki!,* she pointed out that men are more willing to forgive their wives for being unfaithful than for making more money. Al happens not to be one of those. He prays every night that I'll make fifty million dollars a year. Everyone immediately assumes the only reason he's with me is for the money.

And let me tell you, men are far worse about this than

135

women. They say the rudest things to him all the time. "How's it going, Mr. Lawrence?" Or, "So we know what Vicki's doing, what have you been up to?" Or, "What'd you buy lately, Al?"

Or, "What do *you* do for a living?"

Women, on the other hand, tend to love the fact that a man can function effectively as your support team. I'm not good if I'm not working. I never wanted to be just a mom. Maybe that's why I can really appreciate women who spend their lives being full-time mothers, because it's the hardest job in the world. We used to go to hotels and when we'd arrive they'd take my luggage, while security would stop Al to ask, "Where do you think you're going?" or "Who are you?" I always loved when Al would answer, without missing a beat, "I'm her love broker."

A man like Al has to, by necessity, have an infinite amount of patience. I did see him lose it once and actually hit a guy. It happened in 1976, while I was starring in *My Fat Friend,* in Flint, Michigan. The producers threw an opening night press party at a local bar and restaurant, and the cast was obligated to be there. We all went, and Al and I were sitting at a table having a conversation with my leading man, Bob Moak, a major stock star in the Midwest. "Mr. Character Actor."

I noticed these two guys sitting across the room. One of them smoked an entire cigarette without ever taking his eyes off me, and it started to make me really uncomfortable. Finally, he came over and asked if he could have an autograph. I gave him one, and then he wanted to know who the big guy was sitting next to me. "That your bodyguard?"

"No, my husband."

"Bullshit. He's your bodyguard."

The guy went back to his seat, lit up another cigarette, and continued to stare at me. Al was having a great time schmoozing with my cast, and I kept tugging at his sleeve. "Honey? Honey?"

Finally, he said, "For Pete's sake, Vicki, what is the problem?"

That's when I told him this guy was bugging the hell out of me and I wanted to be taken home. Al said, fine, we'll leave.

On the way out, we walked by the guy's table, and now he said he wanted to take our picture. Al said no. The guy called him a Hollywood weirdo and kicked him from under the table. Al looked down at him, noticed the fellow had just put in about two hundred plugs of hair, reached down, picked the guy up by his plugs and threw him into the buffet. Then his friend, who turned out to be his father, attacked Al. I ran and hid. A waitress came over to me and said, "I'm dying to meet you, I'm just so sorry it has to be here behind the salad bar."

I felt like Lady Guinevere as we left the restaurant! My man had fought for my honor! I mean you read about it, you hear about it, guys are always telling their women they would kill for them, but here it had actually happened! I was thrilled!

Al wasn't. "I'm going to be sued," he said. He was right. The next day the father-son tag team filed assault charges against Al and sued him for $10,000. We called an attorney and it turned out because the restaurant had served these people and allowed them to get drunk, they were the ones who had to pay. The assault charges were also dropped when it was discovered the two worked as a team setting up famous people for lawsuits.

Still, as a result we became very gun-shy, wary of trouble. Now, at the first sign of any, we immediately leave.

The silliest things happen in summer stock. I was twenty-two when I first did *Send Me No Flowers*. It was the second season of the Burnett show. Harvey, Lyle, and I were all in the play together. Harvey, who is twenty-two years older than me, was playing my husband.

Harvey never liked to wash his hair, because he was losing it, and thought that washing made it fall out faster.

The problem for me was, it got so disgustingly dirty I couldn't do the kissing scene with him. During one of our final dress rehearsals, I said, "No shit, Harv, wash your hair or the jig's up." He insists to this day every time he washes his hair, he thinks of me. Approximately once a month.

Harvey usually came completely undone before opening night, and this play was no exception. He walked into my dressing room while I was curling my hair, grabbed me, and said, "I know you'll be there for me. I know I can count on you." I finally had to throw him out and force him to take some Librium. I mean he was bouncing all over the place, a complete wreck, prowling the halls reciting Shakespearean warm-ups over and over, *"The moon never beams without bringing me dreams . . ."*

Finally, the play began. In the first scene I'm setting the table for breakfast, I step back and yell offstage, "Breakfast is ready, George," and I can see Harvey standing there in the wings, holding a large card under his nose that said, "I'm not coming out!" What can I say? They don't come any more neurotic than Harvey.

In 1978, I did *Chapter Two* at the Cherry County Playhouse in Traverse City, Michigan. My co-star was Richard Kline, who played that dork on *Three's Company.* Of course, to him I was that dorkette from *The Carol Burnett Show.* As it turned out, there was real chemistry between us. I discovered he was a very well-trained, talented actor, and he was greatly surprised that I could really act. We became great friends.

Al and I were staying in a little condo just outside of Traverse City. After the show one night, I went to wash my face and take my makeup off and noticed that one of the diamond earrings Al had given me for our anniversary was missing. I checked the sink hoping it hadn't gone down the drain. I made Al get out of bed so I could tear the sheets apart, and came up empty. I couldn't figure where I'd lost it. Then I realized it had to be somewhere in the theater.

I rushed back first thing the next morning and there was someone on stage vacuuming. I made him stop immediately until I checked every inch of the floor. Nothing. I got hold of this poor little wardrobe person and together we went through every piece of clothing in the entire theater, and still couldn't find it anywhere. I was devastated.

That night, we were in the middle of the second act's big love scene. The kiss is coming. Richard is acting his ass off. I'm sitting on the carpet with my head on his knee when suddenly I notice an unmistakable sparkle about ten feet from me on the floor. Richard reaches for my chin with his hand. He's going for his kiss, but I'm going for my diamond. I crawled across the stage while Richard ad-libbed I don't know what, I scooted back, the kiss was gone, the audience was laughing, but I didn't care. I had my earring!

I did *My Fat Friend* for several seasons with Bob Moak. Bob's birthday happened to be in the summer. One year I thought I'd buy him something nice. I went down to Carol and Company in Beverly Hills and bought a classic cable-knit, cowl-neck, teddy-bear sweater.

The night of his birthday I took it into his dressing room just before the show and gave it to him. He said, "Oh, I never open gifts in front of people. I just don't. But thank you very much."

I figured maybe he didn't like anything to be made of his birthday. I was a little embarrassed by the whole thing. Later that night I made my first entrance in the second act and there he was, sitting in a wing chair wearing the sweater. I walked on stage, I don't remember what my line was, but instead said, "Oh, what a fabulous sweater!"

"Isn't it delightful," he said. "A very dear friend gave this to me. Do you love it?" Then he got up and modeled it. Right on stage! "It's my birthday, you know!" Sooner or later we did manage to drift back into the play.

One season I did *No, No, Nanette* for the Kenley Circuit of Ohio. Mr. Kenley, bless his soul, I think was a transvestite. One night he told me that he spent his summers as a man and his winters as a woman. "I've even been out to see the Burnett show," he told me, "but because it was winter, you'd never have known it."

He came into my dressing room one time and was fascinated by my hot rollers. The next day he said to me, "I tried those last night. They're fabulous."

"Whatever turns you on, Mr. Kenley," I said. I always called him Mr. Kenley. Ms. would have been too forward.

Anyway, in *No, No, Nanette* my co-stars were Virginia Mayo, Kathleen Freeman, and Gale Gordon, from *The Lucy Show*. That year Mr. Kenley had decided for some reason we all had to rehearse in a tiny little room instead of the local high school gym where we usually did. We had this massive cast, all these dancers, and there was just no way we could all fit in.

It was an altogether hideous week. Mr. Kenley loved to come in and browbeat the hell out of the darling actress who was playing Nanette. Everyone was on edge, and then, to make matters worse, after we opened I got really sick.

We were in Columbus, Ohio, the second city on the circuit. It was ten in the morning and we were all in the theater for a tech rehearsal, when I turned to one of the other cast members and said, "You know, I feel really sick . . ." Someone suggested I get a B_{12} shot from a local doctor.

I got back to the theater just in time for the opening that night, but still felt hideous. The audience was like a blur to me. I couldn't wait to get offstage to the water fountain to have a drink and sit down. At intermission, everyone thought I was drunk.

They took me into my dressing room and started pouring coffee down my throat. "I don't drink," I kept telling them, "I don't ever drink." Still, they kept it up. I don't remember getting through the show.

The next morning I was supposed to drive to Cincinnati for a local TV promotion. I looked in the mirror, and my eyes were so swollen my eyelashes were turning down. I looked like I'd been in the ring with Muhammad Ali! I felt even sicker than before and called Mr. Kenley to tell him I couldn't do the promotion. I couldn't even get out of bed.

"Bullshit," he said. "There's a limousine waiting for you downstairs. You get your ass down there and you get on that road and—"

"You don't understand," I said. "I'm really, really sick." I called Al while they called to have the local hospital have someone come over and do a blood test. The technician they sent was so nervous when he realized I was a celebrity, he came at me holding the needle and shaking like Barney Fife. The blood test confirmed I had mono. They wanted to take me to Cincinnati and put me in the hospital.

I called Al again, this time in tears. "I don't want to die in Ohio. What am I going to do?"

Al said, "Get back in bed and go to sleep, sweetie. I'll come and get you."

I then called Dr. Woods in Los Angeles and kept saying, over and over, "I don't want to die in Ohio."

"You're not going to die," he said. "It's only a three-hour flight home. Take six aspirin, get on the plane, and come see me first thing tomorrow."

Al arrived the next morning. Bless his heart, he was so sweet. While I cried he packed all my stuff for me, took me to the airport, and we got there and sat on the runway forever. The three-hour trip turned into nine. Finally they announced the plane had broken down and we were going to have to wait until they flew in some new equipment from Chicago. As a consolation, they gave everyone free passes to the airport cafeteria. Swell. To pass the time, Al and I played Who Am I? until I'd been everyone I knew.

We finally got home and Al put me to bed. Because I refused to go in the hospital, Dr. Woods came to my house and gave me a shot. Al stayed by my side for two weeks while I slept, woke up, rolled over, and asked for popsicles.

It took six months for me to totally recover. When the Burnett show resumed that fall, the first time I did any sort of dancing at all, I would still get wringing wet, and feel as if I was dying. It took a while and it was not fun.

I never went back to the Kenley Circuit again. I don't think Mr. Kenley ever forgave me. He never really saw me when I was sick, so he never was able to understand just how bad I had gotten.

The question was, where did I get it? I still don't know. The only thing I've ever been able to come up with is that one day I wanted some coffee and Mr. Kenley insisted I drink out of his personal coffee cup. Other than that, I really don't know. And if I did I wouldn't tell. After all, we girls have to stick together.

Garrett, five, Courtney, eight,
visiting their "Mama" on the set.

From Mama to Mom and Back Again to Mama

I have often said I think men can be far more petty game-playing back-stabbers than women. What's more, they love to rag on their wives. Al's got a real good friend who's always on him about our relationship. "How do you spend a week alone with your wife? I can't spend twenty minutes alone with mine." I think the way to avoid all of that is to do what Al and I did—marry your best friend. Every marriage is a roller-coaster ride, love ebbs and flows. You go through periods where it's extremely romantic, and then periods when it's not. A really solid friendship will get you through until the romance returns.

Unfortunately, that wasn't the case with Carol and Joe. All of us who worked with them knew they were, for all intents and purposes, separated long before the divorce.

And when they went through it, they beat the crap out of each other.

It was really sad to watch, and since Joe died, because nothing was cleanly settled, there remains to this day much confusion over rights and residuals connected to *Mama's Family.* I still have not broached the subject with Carol about where that stands these days. As far as I know the only person who gets paid for the Mama character is its owner, Jenna McMahon, one of the original writers of the first skit. Her partner Dick Clair passed away years ago, is currently frozen, and so are his assets. From what I've heard, his residuals go to a cryogenic organization and his family is battling them about it.

During her divorce, Carol and I went through a "cool" period. She "divorced" everyone and remained distant for a lot of years. She called the house a few years ago. I was standing at the sink peeling carrots, fifteen feet from the phone, but Garrett got to it first and I only heard his half of the following conversation: "Hello? Oh hi. Yeah, sure. He's in the other room, on the other line. You want me to tell him you're calling? My mom's here, you want to talk to her? No? Okay. Goodbye."

When he hung up I asked him who it was.

"Carol Burnett."

I was shocked. "What did she say?"

"She didn't want to talk to you. She only wanted to talk to dad."

Al called her back later that night, made a point of telling her how much we missed and loved her, and she told him, "I'll be back. It's just going to take a while longer. Give me another year or so." She went through an incredible amount of pain and adjustment trying to redefine herself after the divorce, and when she finally put it all together, she emerged better and happier for all that had gone down. She was on the *Vicki!* show a lot and remains to this day totally supportive of my career.

*A*fter we finished taping the last Burnett show of the eleventh season, I received a phone call from Carol. She wanted me to know she was ending the show. "I'm not coming back next year and I wanted you to hear it from me before you read it in the press." As a result, there was no final episode, no teary goodbyes, no wrap party, nothing. After eleven years of being on the air, Carol woke up one day and felt she'd done it all, taken the show as far as it could go, and wanted to leave it while she was still on top. I guess you could say she was the Michael Jordan of her day.

I was a little surprised, but ready to make some changes in my life as well. After all, I was twenty-nine, and had done nothing else but *The Carol Burnett Show* since dropping out of UCLA.

I felt that everyday life in Los Angeles had gotten a little too difficult for me. I remember a few weeks after that call, sitting on the Ventura Freeway in bumper-to-bumper traffic. An hour and a half passed and I hadn't gone ten feet. I looked around and saw the same two people on either side of me. I decided to take the steering wheel of the car and see if I could pull it out. I figured, if it came out, I'd have a great story for the Carson show. If it didn't, at least I'd feel better. So I took hold of it and pulled and screamed as hard as I could. Nothing happened. I felt better, looked over and noticed the guy in the next car staring at me. "Fine, thank you. And you?"

"Fine."

*O*nce the show's long run ended, I knocked around for a while, took some auditions, didn't get offered a whole lot, and quickly became disillusioned with the ways of

Hollywood. Casting people either expected me to walk in and, because of Mama, be much older than I was, or arrive in some goofy costume and act like an idiot. There aren't a lot of good projects out there and it's depressing reading one bad script after another.

I did manage to get cast in a couple of pilots that never became series, a lot of game shows, and some dumb guest-star things, like *Fantasy Island* and *The Love Boat.*

Even those came with their share of weirdness. Al's ex-wife, Sherry, was an actress who worked as an extra. When I did an episode of *The Love Boat* one day with my dear friend Richard Kline from summer stock cast as my love interest I discovered she was an extra on it.

The first day of shooting I was on the set when I saw Sherry standing off in one corner, directly in my line of sight, where she stayed during the entire scene. I went to Marge Maret, who was doing our body makeup and happened to be the same woman who did the body makeup on the Burnett show, and asked her what I should do.

"Oh, just ignore her and you'll be fine, honey," she said.

I said, "No, I can't stay here and do this. I just can't. She's driving me nuts." I went to the AD (assistant director) and told him, "I'm going home early."

"You can't do that," he said.

"Well, I am. And tomorrow when I show up for work, if she's here, I'm gone. So you decide who's more important to the show, her or me."

He said, "You can't have one of the extras fired. It's against union rules."

"Have a nice afternoon." And I left. I went out to the parking lot, put my key in the ignition—and fully expected the car to blow up! It didn't, Sherry was gone the next day, and I never heard any repercussions.

After about a year, the vague sensation of being unfulfilled began to come into focus. I realized what the effect of working all those years really was. I simply wanted to be mom for a while, instead of "Mama." I was pretty much fed up with Hollywood, and since both Al and I were so in love with Hawaii, in 1979 we sold literally everything we had but the kids and moved there.

This meant leaving Hidden Hills. When we'd first found this spot up in the San Fernando Valley north of Hollywood, it was a quiet ranch community. There were still horse trails, and every property had to have a six-foot easement for them. We fell in love with the area.

During the two years we lived there, we became very close friends with our neighbors. One day shortly after we moved in a fellow by the name of Bob Crystal came up, knocked on our door, introduced himself and told us that his family was moving into the house across the street. Somehow it came up that he was Jewish. Al said, "You see that horse trail over there?"

"Yeah?"

"Well, that's the Gaza Strip."

Bob laughed hysterically, and that was the start of a beautiful friendship, to the point where we're in each other's wills. If one of us dies the others get the kids. Thank God theirs are grown.

When we decided to move to Hawaii, we put the house up for sale. Bob told us we were crazy to sell it. "Why don't you just rent it," he said, "and lease something over there for a year." As it turned out, he was right, but at the time we just wanted to cut all our apron strings and get out of L.A., we thought forever.

Al had introduced me to Hawaii. Because he had always gone to Waikiki with his ex-wife, he was anxious to find a new spot. We decided to try Maui. When we first arrived it looked to me like something out of *Gidget Goes Hawaiian*, right down to this cool little bar at the beach, in the sand. What can I say, I thought I had died and gone to heaven.

One day we were driving around and wound up at Kapalua. It was so beautiful Al and I walked into a tiny sales office, met the real estate agent, Bob Sullivan, who took us out to this point where he told us condos were going to be built. We looked at the ocean, then at each other, and said, "Sign us up." All the locals there call Kapalua "Seattle" because it rains so often. Of course, if you're there a great deal, it's nice to have a break from the sun. We knew we were going to love it in our little condo in "Seattle."

We were responsible for bringing Carol to Maui as well, who, in turn, brought Jim Nabors. Carol and Joe had always preferred the Big Island, until their favorite spot, the Mauna Kea Hotel, changed hands. Because they knew that Al and I loved Maui so much, they decided to give it a try.

We encouraged them to come to Kapalua but they chose the other side of the island instead. Because it was Easter and also my birthday, Carol and Joe invited us to dinner. Unfortunately, it was also spring vacation, and the place was a zoo.

Carol was mobbed. I remember going into the ladies' room with her, and people shoving paper underneath our stalls, saying, "Could you sign this?" It was ridiculous! They were standing there with flash cameras waiting for us when we came out. That's when I grabbed Carol and said that she really had to see Kapalua.

The next day they drove over, Al had a golf game set up for Joe, who was a golf nut, after which they came back to the condo. Carol walked through to the lanai, looked out on the ocean, turned to Joe and said, "If you love me, you'll buy me one of these."

They purchased two units in The Ironwoods, an exclusive development that had just broken ground, and made a huge, gorgeous place out of it for themselves. It became Joe's favorite place until the day he died.

· · ·

*M*aui would prove an interesting, if short-lived adventure for us. At first it seemed positively idyllic, especially for the children. We put Garrett in the Kapalua preschool, an adorable, picturesque converted missionary church. His teachers were all Hawaiian, and when we'd drop him off in the morning they'd say, "Aloha, Garrett, *ka-ka hiaka* (good morning)!"

School trips meant going to the beach to dig for seashells. We'd pick him up in the afternoon and he'd be sacked out on his little mat, with a soft warm breeze blowing, and I'd say that little guy has no idea how lucky he is!

Things were a little more complicated with Courtney. The only school we could get her into was a forty-five-minute drive each way. It was either that, or board her, which I couldn't bear to do. Then Al managed to pull some strings and got her into a Catholic school only fifteen minutes away in Lahaina. Still, it was a far from perfect solution. We weren't Catholic, not even close. When she came home with ashes on her forehead, I started wondering what the lesson was that day.

One afternoon Courtney came home from school and announced that she'd made a new friend who lived near the school and wanted to know if she could have her out to the condo to play that weekend. I was very happy about this, said sure, and asked if she had a phone number so I could call the child's mother.

When I got the woman on the phone I discovered she didn't speak English very well. I tried to explain to her that the girls wanted to play over the weekend.

"Pray?"

"Play. How about Saturday?"

"Party?"

"Play."

"Pray?"

This went on for about twenty minutes, during which I also tried to get directions from her so I could come and pick her daughter up. All I was able to make out was "water tower," "Howard Johnson's," and "sugarcane factory." I hung up the phone and asked Al what I should do. He suggested we call Bob Sullivan, who'd lived on the island since the end of World War Two. Al figured if anyone would know where we should go, he would. I called, got his wife, Paula, on the phone and asked her what she could make out of the "clues."

Her initial reaction was, "Oh my God. They're Filipino."

"What does that mean?"

"They live back in the cane fields. You're not going to let Courtney play with their little girl, are you?"

"Why not? She sounds sweet and Courtney really likes her. I'm happy she's made a friend."

"They eat dogs, Vicki."

"*What?*"

"You know those big black dogs they raise and keep in those cages back there? They eat them."

"That's disgusting!"

That Saturday morning, Al and I drove to the Filipino village behind the sugarcane field, and the people there looked at us like we were howling idiots. It was an instant flashback to Vietnam for me. We couldn't see the village from the road, because it was literally behind the factory, smack in the middle of the cane fields. You wouldn't know there was anybody there unless you knew where you were going, past the muddy roads, to the Quonset huts, complete with old guys smoking Marlboros in rocking chairs on porches.

By the time we found the little girl's house, I had begun to wonder what we'd gotten ourselves into. Then, these two adorable little girls, starched and pressed to the nines, emerged with their mother. I promised to return them before dark, and off we went.

Those darling kids didn't want to play with anything in Courtney's room, they just wanted to touch it all. They wanted to look at every page of every book, every doll, every dress. When we went out to the swimming pool, the younger of the two girls just jumped in and started to sink to the bottom.

"*AL!*"

He had to literally walk into the pool, go down the steps, grab her by the hair and pull her up. "My God," I said. "She doesn't know how to swim!"

"Of course not," Al said. "She's used to wading in the ocean. What does she know about swimming pools."

For lunch, I made the girls peanut butter and jelly sandwiches, with potato chips. They refused to touch it. I thought to myself, hey, you eat dogs, don't you? What's wrong with this?

We decided to sell our little condo and plunk down a ton of money on one of The Ironwoods condos across the street from Carol and Joe. We were so close I could go to her house to borrow a cup of sugar. The kids loved Carol, and she always had cookies for them and lots of fun things for them to do. Sometimes, though, they drove her nuts. Finally, she devised a little signal for them; if there was a red ribbon on the door they could knock. If there was no ribbon she was to be left alone.

Both Al and I had longtime dreams we wanted to live out in Maui. I always thought it would be fun to run a boutique. I'm a confessed shopaholic and it was my ultimate fantasy to travel all over Europe buying clothes for my store and *getting everything wholesale.* Because there are only T-shirts and muumuus in Maui, I thought I might be able to bring some style to the island. Al, meanwhile, had always thought Maui needed a great steakhouse. The best beef, his homemade chili, man-sized drinks.

The only problem was, at the time we lived there the economy wasn't in such great shape, and before long we started to see things more realistically, including what it took to live full-time on Maui.

Logistically, it's very hard to live on a little island after you've been used to a big city your whole life. The cost of living is twice as expensive, and if you can afford it, twice as difficult. Going to an orthodontist means getting on a plane and flying to Honolulu. And there's no such thing as, hey, let's go to the ballet. The ballet may come to Honolulu once every nine months and you have to fly there to see it.

Then there was the small-town thing. Everybody knew everything we did, what we ate for dinner the night before, when we had a fight, everything.

Every time Courtney went horseback riding at the stable in the mountains, her head would get full of lice. I'd have to get RID and treat her with it. If you've never had the pleasure, the deal is it will kill the lice, but if you leave it on too long your hair will start to fall out. Mother called one night as I was in the middle of delicing Courtney's head.

"My God, Vicki," she said. "You never had anything like that! How could you let this happen!" Like I was the worst mother that ever lived!

Finally, I wasn't getting a lot of job offers. You can have a ranch in Montana, or live in New York, and people will call you from L.A. every minute, but if you're in Hawaii they tend to leave you alone. People think when you live in Hawaii you're sitting on the beach with a pitcher of mai-tais and do not want to be bothered. So when I got a call to ask if I'd be interested in doing another episode of *Love Boat*, I was on the next plane back to the mainland.

My favorite story about doing *Love Boat* is when I was cast with Misty Rowe, and we played sisters. In the script, she had a little thing going with Bernie Kopell, the ship's doctor, and was bringing her pitiful, forlorn sister who had just broken up with someone along for the cruise.

That was me, and I ended up ruining their romance at every turn.

When I first saw Misty, very sexy, very blonde, talks in a sweet, little girl voice, I thought to myself, oh yeah, we look like sisters. The first day of shooting she came over to me and said, "I just hate how long it takes between shots! Would you like to play some backgammon with me?"

"Yeah, I'll play backgammon with you," I said, wondering how she even knew such a big word. She pulled out a portable backgammon board. I asked how we were going to roll the dice without making any noise.

"No prob*lem!* Electronic dice!"

"Well," I said, "that's really cute. Where did you get that?"

"Hef gave it to me!"

Well, okay! To make a long story short, she beat the crap out of me. Every single game. The woman was unbelievable! She was like Judy Holliday in *Born Yesterday.* When we began, she suggested we play for a quarter a point, and by the end of the week I owed her my paycheck!

Misty and I became really good friends. We went shopping a lot together, and it was amazing to watch her with salesmen. She got anything she wanted! Later on, after Al and I moved back to Los Angeles, Misty invited us over several times for dinner at her place up in the Hollywood Hills. It was a fun house, filled with Marilyn Monroe memorabilia. She's a fabulous cook, and a great hostess. She used to do this great thing at dinner, which I absolutely loved. She would take a Polaroid when you walked through the door, then when you sat down to dinner there'd be a lovely framed picture of you in front of your place setting; a fabulous memento of the evening.

One night, we were at her house having a wonderful Southern dinner and I went into the kitchen to see if I could help with anything. Out of this sort of invisible panel in the wall a door opened and a little man came out. It was her grandfather, who was ill. Misty explained to us that nobody else in her family seemed to want him, so she had this little room added over the garage for grandpa. That's the kind of person she is.

Anyway, so I came in to do that *Love Boat* with Misty, and left Al in Hawaii with the kids. As we were about to start shooting, a huge rash suddenly broke out on my face. It was burning and itching and I couldn't get rid of it. I had never been to a dermatologist before. As I was sitting in his office waiting to see him, I told the nurse that at thirty I thought I'd outgrown this stuff.

"Are you kidding," she said. "Thirty to forty is a horrible time in your life for stress and usually the prime time for acne."

The doctor confirmed the rash was a symptom of the enormous stress I was feeling and it took forever to get rid of it. This was midway through our year living in Hawaii, just as we began to realize we no longer had any desire to run our own businesses, and were bored to death. Neither one of us wanted to say anything to the other, but we both knew we had made a mistake.

It would be some four months later when Al finally spoke the unspeakable. One night while we were watching television, he said to me, "I don't know about you, but I am so unhappy living here."

"Me too."

That was it. For the next two weeks Al took care of everything while I did nothing but cry. He packed us up and made all the arrangements to move us off the island and back to Los Angeles.

Not that it had been uniformly awful or we wouldn't have lasted there for even as long as we did. There were lots of fun times and great discoveries. We visited frequently; in fact, the following summer I took the kids over and waited while Al did Transpac, the semi-annual L.A. to Honolulu yacht race. Al and eight crew set sail from the mainland in July 1981 on our racing sloop, *Oz.*

Cathy Fisher, a girlfriend of mine from Michigan, came over to Hawaii to stay with me when her husband decided to join Al's crew that year. I'll never forget, we were sitting by the pool one day, Cath had her big straw hat over her head, and I decided to go inside and call headquarters to find out how the guys were doing. Every day they have to call in and report, and I could call Transpac central for an update. That morning I was told the *Oz* was reported sinking.

"I beg your pardon?"

"At six-fifty-five the yacht *Oz* reported it was sinking, and needed help. At six-fifty-nine a C-130 was loaded up and—"

"Wait a minute!"

" . . . at seven-oh-two the request was canceled. They said they were fine."

"That's it?"

I went out to Cath and told her about the messages. "They're not sinking," she said. "Besides, there's five hundred boats out there. They'll be fine." The thing is, once you ask for assistance you're out of the race. What had happened, we found out later, was that the *Oz* had nose-dived under a wave, popped out backward, and had taken on so much water they flipped on the bilge pump. Unbeknownst to Al and his crew, the pump had been installed the wrong way, and they were actually pumping *in* something like twenty-eight gallons of water a minute, until someone suggested they turn the bilge pump off and they stopped sinking.

In spite of everything they finished first in their class but corrected out to fourth place. It was a wonderful experience. So much so that we're in the process of building a new boat now, and when it's finished we're going to do

155

Transpac in it together, something that not many people get to do.

Anyway, we wound up living in Maui for less than a year. I know this because we had a ton of friends over for Thanksgiving two days after we moved to Hawaii. I got off the plane and headed straight for the kitchen. When we moved back to L.A., it was two weeks before Thanksgiving. Once again, I got off a plane and headed straight for a kitchen.

But that was okay. I didn't mind at all. We were happy to be back in civilization. We eventually sold our Ironwood and developed a whole new appreciation for the Ventura Freeway.

By this time we had had a fair number of homes. Besides the condo in Maui, there was that first house in Sherman Oaks, which we sold when we moved to the new development off Benedict Canyon, where we lived for about two years before we bought the big house in Hidden Hills. We stayed there for another two and a half years before Maui. Upon our return, we leased a place in Malibu Colony for several months, then returned to Hidden Hills. Al said he thought it would be great for the kids to be able to return to their original schools. He made a really good deal for a little ranch house on the other end of the same area we had lived in before.

No sooner had we moved in when early in 1982 I made another "return" of sorts, to weekly television, in *Mama's Family*.

The idea for the series had originated in 1975. One day, shortly after Courtney was born, Joe came down and sat next to me in the empty audience during a Burnett show rehearsal. "You're going to have your own series, Vicki," he said. "We're going to spin off Mama into a sitcom for

CBS, and Dick and Jenna are going to be the head writers. Isn't that exciting?"

My first reaction was, what about Harvey and Carol?

He said, "I don't think you need them."

I wasn't so sure about that. Besides, I wasn't ready to play a fat old woman every week. I'd just given birth to Courtney. I'd been fat for nine months.

"Look," Joe said, "this is the opportunity of a lifetime."

"Yes, but what if it fails?"

"Then we'll bring you back here."

"I get to come back with my tail tucked between my legs?"

"That's not the way to look at it."

"What about Carol? She won't be able to use those characters on her own show anymore."

He got exasperated, left, and didn't speak to me again for a week. I was hoping Carol wasn't going to be upset with me as well. I soon found out how much she wasn't when I saw her come down the hall a couple of hours after that first conversation with Joe looking just radiant. "Sweetie," she said, "I'm so happy you made the decision not to do Mama, because that means we can keep doing it on this show." Okay, I figured. Fine.

The idea for the show didn't come up again for five years, until 1980, after the Burnett show had left the air Both Carol and I were in Hawaii. I was by the pool, lying facedown on a chaise, when she came by and threw a script down in front of me.

I looked up.

"Read it and tell me what you think."

"What is it?"

"Just read it."

Dick and Jenna had written a ninety-minute movie-of-the-week based on "The Family" sketches, entitled *Eunice.* I thought it was terrific, except for one thing. Mama died at the end. When I mentioned this to Carol, she laughed,

"You're so greedy! Do you want to do this or not?"

We shot *Eunice* in spring 1981. Not long after, Carol called and invited Al and me and the cast up to her house to have dinner and watch a screening of the show. As we were driving up to her house, Al, my half-Greek psychic, said, "You know what's going to happen tonight? Carol is going to ask you to do Mama as a series."

We ate, sat down to watch that special, and no sooner did the credits start to roll when Carol, Joe, and Harvey were all over me like a bad suit. "You have to do this as a series," Joe insisted, promising me he would take care of everything. Carol and Harvey both assured me they would come and guest on it. Later on, Carol took me aside and said, "You do this for five years and you can do whatever you want for the rest of your life."

Eunice aired on March 15, 1982 and placed among the top ten most popular shows of that week.

For my portrayal of Mama, I was nominated for an Emmy in the category of Outstanding Supporting Actress in a Limited Series or a Special. Before the show actually aired, I got a really neat note from Carol, in which she wrote, *"I'm so proud of you, I can't stand it! You're the best young actress-comedienne in this whole damn country. You put the show in your pocket and I couldn't be happier! I love you, Carol."*

Still, I was one goofy old lady up against some pretty stiff competition, among them Claire Bloom for *Brideshead Revisited,* Judy Davis for *A Woman Named Golda,* Rita Moreno for *Portrait of a Showgirl,* and Penny Fuller for *The Elephant Man.* When I asked Harvey what he thought my chances were of winning, he laughed and said, "No fucking way!" He was right. Penny Fuller went home with the trophy.

Even so, Al and I thought, if *Mama's Family* was a hit, we would be sitting on easy beach, sipping margaritas, while we figured out what we wanted to do next.

From Mama to Mom and Back Again to Mama

It was a hard decision to make. A lot of people at the time said I shouldn't do it, that the series would typecast me, and to a degree I think that did happen. To this day, people say to me, "You're so much younger than we thought you were." One night last year there was a woman in the audience of my talk show with a very thick Italian accent who said she saw me every night in Italy, but I looked so old and fat on TV.

On the other hand, I wasn't getting a lot of wonderful offers. I'd get scripts from agents who would say a producer specifically wanted me for a role, thought I'd be perfect, I'd read it, and not know whether to be offended by it or laugh!

Once I signed things began to reverberate with a familiar vibe. For instance, I said to Al one day, "You know how Linda Lavin sings her own theme song on *Alice?* Wouldn't it be fun for me to sing mine?" Al agreed. So I wrote the lyrics and mapped out a theme for *Mama's Family* and took it to Peter Matz, who was the musical director Joe had hired for the show. Peter refined it, wrote it all out, and arranged it. We then went in and recorded it, and when I asked Joe what I would be getting for it, he said, "You want money for this?"

I said, "Yes, that would be nice." He said he could write something better on the toilet in five minutes. That was his charming way of saying no.

So Peter got full credit for the music, I never got even half credit, Joe refused to use the lyrics, and of course I never got paid a nickel. The show went with an instrumental version of the song, and that was the end of that. On the credit roll at the end of every show is my theme title, my name for the song, "Bless My Happy Home," and no mention that I wrote it.

Grant Tinker, then the head of programming at NBC, had given Joe a direct on-air, no-pilot green light. However, after the first two tapings, it was clear to Al and me that the show wasn't working. Joe shut us down for six weeks while we tried to fix what had gone wrong. A key

> CAROL BURNETT
>
> May 25, 1981
>
> My Darling Wick —
>
> Well — we did it.
> I'm so proud of you, I can't stand it!
> You're the best young actress-comedienne
> in this whole damn country —
> you put the show in your pocket
> and I couldn't be happier!
> See you at home.
>
> I love you
> Carol

move we made was to get Harvey Korman to help with the comic staging.

As usual, Harvey was brilliant. One of the first things he said was that you can't expect people to come home after a hard day at the office and sit down to watch someone like Mama scream and yell for a half hour. In the context of the Burnett show, where the sketch was more slice-of-life, one-dimensional, and vaudevillian, you could get away with it. Harvey insisted we now had to make Mama a real person. She needed to be more colorful, he said, and to have a spectrum of emotions. She couldn't go around just screaming and frowning all the time.

I wasn't sure. "That's all I know," I told Harvey. "Mama doesn't laugh, and Mama can't smile."

"You smile," he said. "You laugh. You *are* Mama!"

God, that was a frightening thought.

1. Mom—Ann Alene Loyd—at her high school graduation.

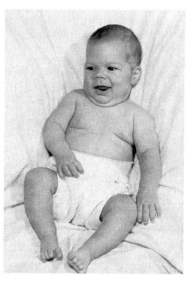

3. Me at six months. Notice the "club foot"? No? Neither do I!

2. Major Howard Lawrence, my dad.

4. Me at three.

5. Joni (she's one) and me (I'm seven), when we still got a

7. My winning essay and my chemistry set,
   the prize that nearly blew up the house.

8. "Young Americans." That's me in the bottom front row far right.

9. Miss Fireball hugging her new best friend.

10. Learning about the important things in life from Lyle.

11. John Davidson—one of my first crushes.

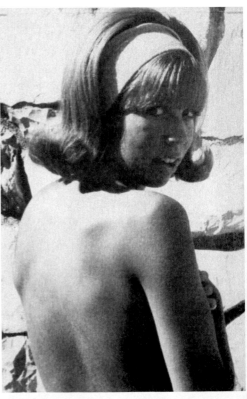

12. My Vietnam pinup.

13. A sunburned evening out in Vietnam. L to R: OB, Karen, The Brass, me, Melody, and Johnny Grant.

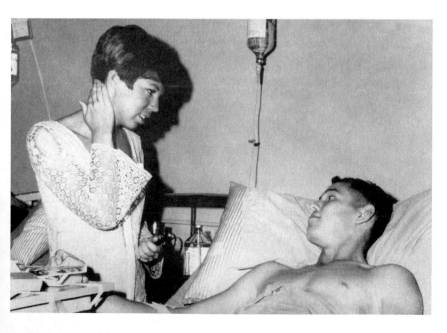

15. Visiting a wounded soldier.

16. With Don on the *Jimmy Rogers Summer Show*. "What lines!"

17. The image of Bobby I fell in love with.

LITTLE GREEN APPLES
Words and Music by **BOBBY RUSSELL**

BEST SONG OF THE YEAR

18. With Harvey, doing *Send Me No Flowers* in summer stock, 1970.

19. Oy! Our wedding day.

20. With Duffy, the only thing I kept from my first marriage.

21. Our wedding day. With a bun in my oven and Al on the throne.

22. The reception. Al on codeine with a champagne chaser.

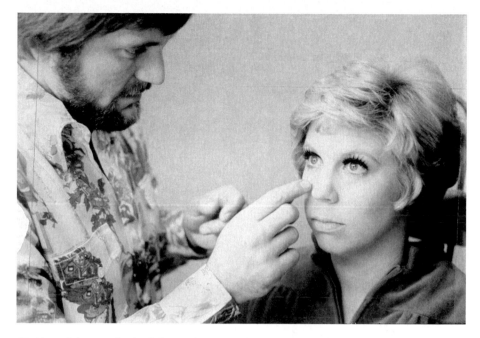

23. The eighth season finale of *The Carol Burnett Show*.   The head of CBS makeup gave me good face.

24. Joni doing my makeup on *Mama's Family*. She was still speaking to me.

Use this key to identify the CBS stars in the accompanying photograph.

1	Lassie	29	Bonnie Franklin	59	Sherman Hemsley	85	Glen Campbell
2	Jean Stapleton	30	William Conrad	60	Jack Whitaker	86	Buddy Ebsen
3	Walter Cronkite	31	Eva Gabor	61	Isabel Sanford	87	Michael Learned
4	Alfred Hitchcock	32	Allen Funt	62	Judy Norton-Taylor	88	John Forsythe
5	Mary Tyler Moore	33	Tim Conway	63	Bob Denver	89	Steve Allen
6	Ellen Corby	34	Danny Thomas	64	Carroll O'Connor	90	Carol Burnett
7	Gene Rayburn	35	Bob Keeshan	65	Dwayne Hickman	91	Jim Nabors
8	Vivian Vance	36	Dennis Weaver	66	Richard C. Hottelet	92	Beatrice Arthur
9	Milburn Stone	37	Ray Walston	67	Will Geer	93	Loretta Swit
10	Ann Sothern	38	Sally Struthers	68	Lesley Stahl	94	Ed Bradley
11	Barbara Bain	39	Garry Moore	69	Art Carney	95	Andy Griffith
12	Nancy Walker	40	Linda Lavin	70	Tony Randall	96	Lee Meriwether
13	George Burns	41	Douglas Edwards	71	Bob Newhart	97	Demond Wilson
14	Cicely Tyson	42	Betty White	72	Dick Smothers	98	Lynda Carter
15	Arthur Godfrey	43	Bob Schieffer	73	Hughes Rudd	99	James Arness
16	Red Skelton	44	Ned Beatty	74	Ted Knight	100	Dick Van Dyke
17	Gale Storm	45	Charles Kuralt	75	Georgia Engel	101	Jack Lord
18	Danny Kaye	46	Arlene Francis	76	Jon Walmsley	102	Ralph Waite
19	Sandy Duncan	47	Jamie Farr	77	Charles Collingwood	103	Bernard Kalb
20	Telly Savalas	48	Adrienne Barbeau	78	Audrey Meadows	104	Martin Landau
21	Dale Evans	49	Vicki Lawrence	79	Valerie Harper	105	Rob Reiner
22	Roy Rogers	50	Mary McDonough	80	Julie Kavner	106	Lynnie Greene
23	Ken Murray	51	Don Knotts	81	David Harper	107	John Amos
24	June Lockhart	52	Lucille Ball	82	Bill Macy	108	Bob Barker
25	Arthur Murray	53	Edward Asner	83	Ken Berry	109	Bert Convy
26	Kathryn Murray	54	Jackie Cooper	84	Art Linkletter	110	Dan Rather
27	Eric Scott	55	Esther Rolle			111	Richard Crenna
28	Kami Cotler	56	Joan Hackett			112	Mike Connors
		57	Eric Sevareid			113	David Groh
		58	Mike Wallace				

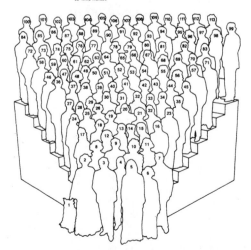

25. CBS's 50th Anniversary photo (I'm number 49).

27. The 1993 *Carol Burnett Reunion Show*.

29. The Schultz family today.

30. Carol and "Sis." Notice I"m doing my best Carol Burnett impersonation.

32. The first show: Carol always called Jim Nabors her lucky charm.

33. Carol, me, and Bernadette Peters. A World War II musical takeoff. Which twin has the "Toni"?

34. Me, Carol, Jimmy Rodgers, and Lyle. The last *Carol Burnett Show* of the 1968-69 season. It was on this show that Carol handed her time slot over to Jimmy for the summer.

35. Branching out to new characters.

36. Me, Carol, and Harvey. A couple of Girl Scout cookies.

37. "The Doily Sisters," 1972.

38. Me with my dreaded Afro dancing with, L to R: Stan Mazin and Randy Doney, two of the show's regular dancers.

39. Carol as Groucho, me as Harpo, Harvey as Chico. Doing the Marx brothers.

40. Me introing one of our classic movie takeoffs.

41. Early "Mama." Notice the showgirl eyes.

43. Fall 1975. With Tim and Harvey.

44. The People's Choice Award, 1978. Our last season. L to R: Joe Hamilton, me, Carol, Tim Conway.

45. Me turning into "Mama," 1980.

46. The original NBC cast.
Clockwise starting with me:
Karen Argood, Dorothy Lyman,
Ken Berry, Eric Brown,
Rue McLanahan.

48. The only actress in showbiz who goes to makeup to get ugly.

49. The syndicated cast. Top row, L to R: Allan Kayser, Ken Berry. Seated, L to R: Beverly Archer, me, Dorothy Lyman.

50. Keeping Vinton in line.

51. Studying for my high
school equivalency diploma.

52. All tied up.

53. "Mama" visits "Vicki!" That's her, second from left.

54. Al and me at the mansion with Hef!

55. With Garth Brooks.

56. With Fess Parker.

57. Al's fantasies. Go figure.

58. L to R: Ann Miller, Janet Leigh, Mickey Rooney, me, June Allyson, Gloria DeHaven.

59. Dick Clark, Harvey, and me.

60. "The Men in My Life." L to R: Snuff Garrett, Dick Clark, Lyle, Al, Ken, my dad, me,
Garrett, and Mr. Happy-Go-Lucky.

61. With Dinah.

63. "Vicki's Crushes." L to R: Jan and Dean, John Davidson, Al, Jimmy Darren, Lyle.

65. Sally Kirkland enjoying my controversial breastplate.

66. Singing "Georgia" with Reba.

67. Sumo wrestling. Can you tell which one is padded?

68. Cocktails with Doris Day.

From Mama to Mom and Back Again to Mama

It was a difficult transition for me to make. However, once I learned how to make Mama laugh, there was nothing she couldn't get away with. The only time I got into an argument with our writers was over a script where Mama's dead husband's brother came to visit. He was a merchant marine, they hadn't seen each other in years, and Mama and this guy ended up in bed together.

I knew this was wrong. Mama is nothing if not Bible Belt, where, even if your husband is dead, you don't sleep with his brother. That must be in the Bible somewhere. I insisted on a rewrite for the entire second half of the script, and this one time Joe was solidly behind me. I knew the character better than anybody, he said. If I thought something was wrong, something had to be wrong.

The way the episode finally turned out, the family only *thought* they had slept together, but she couldn't go through with it. Prior to this, I would get a script on Monday morning like everybody else and go to the regular meeting. Now I said to Joe, "You know, I think it would be much better for me if I could get scripts a week early, so if there's something that's really wrong, I could say so and the writers could have a jump on making the changes."

And Joe, God love him, said, "Absolutely not. Actors can't think about two scripts at once. End of discussion."

Once again, it was obvious to me he didn't understand women. We think about *eight zillion things* at once. Our job, the kids, dinner, homework, husbands, PTA, recycling, the nuclear holocaust. Throw an extra script in the mix, what the hell is that?

Like the Burnett show, *Mama* was shot in four-camera "live-on-tape" style; we taped twice, for two different audiences, and edited the best of both shows together. And like the Burnett show, we taped at CBS, even though *Mama's Family* originally ran on NBC. By this time, the studios had gotten to the point where they didn't care who

161

rented space, as long as it was rented. Besides, Joe wanted to use stage 33, because that's where he had produced the Burnett show, which freaked me out. I would have much preferred to get as far away from that stage as possible.

We had all the same camera people and crew as well, and I was in Carol's dressing room, feeling a lot of pressure when Joe said he wanted me to go out and warm up the audience, doing questions and answers before the actual taping, *just like Carol used to.* I found myself thrown into a hell of a big spotlight.

Our original NBC time slot was opposite *The Love Boat* on ABC, which was a very popular show. When we started building an audience and getting really good numbers, the network decided to move us. We wound up opposite *Magnum P.I.,* where we got slammed once more until we started building up numbers. Then NBC moved us again. It finally dawned on me the network was going to keep moving us around until they could justify canceling us.

In spite of Grant Tinker's support, I think the young honchos at NBC really resented us. Number one, they didn't understand rural comedy. Number two, their mantra in those pre–Bill Cosby days was "Sitcoms don't work anymore." Number three, they didn't get why a young woman was playing an old woman. And number four, they didn't particularly like Joe, who was not what you would describe as your basic diplomat. He had this funny little habit of telling people to fuck off. As a result, after only thirty-five shows we were canceled.

A year later, Lorimar, a major syndicator, took a look at us, particularly our demographics, and said, "This show should have been a hit. It just never got a fair shake." Joe put together a lucrative first-run syndication deal for himself with Lorimar.

However, when it came time to sign the cast, he pleaded poverty. His initial offer to me was an 80 percent cut in salary from what I had been making when we were on the network, take-it-or-leave-it. His explanation? "It's syndication, we have no budget." I told him to stick it.

I asked Harvey what he thought I should do, and he said, "Vicki, you need a good agent to negotiate this one."

He was right, only I didn't have a good agent, a bad agent, or any agent at all, not since Mike Ovitz had abandoned me. So Harvey introduced me to his: Tony Fantozzi of the William Morris Agency, with whom I wound up signing.

I liked him and I was impressed with the big bucks he'd gotten Harvey when the Burnett show went into syndication. To pressure Joe, Harvey and Fantozzi threatened to literally shut the whole deal down. They not only flat out refused Joe's initial low offer, but they called a major press conference at one of the big hotels in Beverly Hills. After a couple of martinis, Harvey got up to speak and asked the unions not to sanction the show because it was unfair to its supporting players. The next day Joe quietly sweetened Harvey's deal.

What it had all come down to was that abusive Tinseltown mind-set when it comes to actors and actresses. The notion that we're expendable is as old as Hollywood itself. That's one of the reasons why, as much as I was anxious to get back to work, I was determined not to cave in when Joe decided to play hardball with me.

Not long after refusing Joe's offer, I received a letter from his office saying, "We've decided to go ahead with the series and recast Mama."

I wrote back telling him to go for it, and suggested he get Tim Conway to play her in drag. Not long after, Lee Rich, the head of Lorimar, asked Fantozzi, Al, and me to lunch at the Beverly Hills Hotel, where he promised to restructure my deal in a far more favorable and fair fashion. Well, I fell immediately in love with Lee and thought he was the nicest man I'd ever met.

He kept his word, worked out a fair deal with Fantozzi for me. One key element was that I no longer would be working for Joe Hamilton, but for Lorimar directly. I was also able to negotiate for a staff that would be able to support me and make the show that much better. One of the first things I wanted was for Rick Hawkins to be hired as the head writer and producer. We'd grown up together on *The Carol Burnett Show*. He was my age, he was Southern, and he understood Mama almost as well as I did. We also brought in Dave Powers, the director of the Burnett show.

A funny thing happened the day I signed with Lorimar. Carol called and said, "I think I'd like to put together maybe a little syndicated show with the *family* characters. I'll do Eunice, you do Mama. Doesn't that sound like fun?"

I said, "It does, but I just signed with Lorimar to do *Mama's Family* for Joe."

It became a very abrupt conversation, and Carol hung up. I then went in to Al and asked him what he made of the whole thing. He agreed it was really weird. I wondered if I was about to get caught in the middle of yet another struggle between the two of them. I would much rather have worked for Carol than Joe. No. Let me amend that. I would much rather have worked for *anybody* than Joe.

We did twenty-two new episodes a year in syndication over a five-year period. The best thing about first-run syndication, and the reason I believe the shows we did that way were better than the original thirty-five we did for the network, was that we didn't have all those suits constantly on our backs.

The down part of syndication is, you really don't belong to anybody. You're like an orphan child, it's hard to get the cover of *TV Guide* or the Sunday supplements because your time slot varies from city to city.

When we went back into production, the only other sitcom in first-run syndication was Ted Knight's *Too Close for Comfort,* which was then retitled *The Ted Knight Show,* and which did very well. Ted became my role model. I figured if he could do it, maybe I could too. It was a tremendous feeling of triumph and vindication when almost immediately *Mama's Family* became the number one sitcom in syndication, where we stayed for the rest of our run.

I was up in San Francisco two years ago for a broadcasters' convention, and Brandon Tartikoff happened to be sitting across from Al and me at the hotel where we were staying. He left the people he was with to come over and say, "I have to tell you a funny story. I'm living down in New Orleans to be with my daughter while she recuperates from her automobile accident, and I absolutely love to laugh at the late-night wars between Letterman, Arsenio, and Jay. In New Orleans, between ten and eleven, when the networks air these shows down there, the local channel runs two episodes of *Mama's Family* back-to-back. Leno's doing something like a 4 rating, Arsenio's a 3, Letterman a 6, and *Mama*'s pulling a 10! I read the ratings every week and just howl!"

That's been true for a number of markets. In some, they put us on in prime time, two episodes back-to-back, and we regularly kill the network prime-time competition. I fully believe that Mama could run for governor down South and win.

One of my favorite trivia questions for Mama fans is, "Can you name all the members of Mama's family from the Burnett show through the sit-com?" I'm not even sure I have it straight, but here goes. Carol was always Eunice, Betty White was always Ellen. Harvey was always Ed Higgins, and Tim was always Mickey Hart. Those actors and characters are pretty well ingrained in our memories. I had a number of other children on the Burnett show. Alan Alda once guested as one of my sons, as did Tommy Smothers. The last season of the Burnett show, Dick Van Dyke had a somewhat recurring role in the family.

When we went to the special, it was all the mainstay characters, Ed, Eunice, Mama, Betty White's character Ellen, and Philip, my son, the role that Roddy McDowall had originated on the Burnett show. When he proved un-available for the special, Carol got her second choice to take over the role, Ken Berry. Remember, Mama died in the special, and, like Bobby Ewing on *Dallas,* was totally reborn for the series.

When we went to NBC, the cast was me; Ken Berry now playing a new character, Vinton, my son; Dorothy Lyman was his wife, Naomi; Rue McClanahan was my sister, Fran. There were two kids, Buzz and Sonja, played by Eric Brown and Karin Argoud. They were added because NBC wanted the show to have some appeal to teenagers. Finally, Betty White made occasional appearances as Ellen, my lovely daughter.

Between the time that we were canceled by NBC and went into syndication, Betty White and Rue McClanahan both left to do *The Golden Girls.* The first thing Joe did in syndication was to lose the teenagers. He did agree to add a new character, Mama's grandson, so the show would still have a young person. We hired Allan Kayser to play Bubba. We added a new neighbor, Iola, played by Beverly Archer, to replace my sister. Dorothy and Ken came back. As a result of all the changes, the syndicated cast was stronger than the original. *Whew!*

*J*oe passed away in 1991. It wasn't pretty. While we were still doing *Mama's Family* he was diagnosed as hav-ing a tumor behind one of his eyes. As a result, the tumor, eye, part of his forehead, and most of his cheek had to be surgically removed. They can do all kinds of things with leather patches and prosthetics that would have made him look all right, but he would have none of it. He'd come in once a week, I guess because he wanted to remain active. Before coming down from his office to the readings, he'd go into the restroom, get a paper towel and improvise a patch that covered half his face. His whole life he was a compulsive smoker, and even after the surgery he refused to give it up. During the meetings he'd light up a cigarette and the smoke would escape from the edges of the paper towel. It looked as if his head were smoldering. It was real difficult for all of us to have to see.

The way I found out he died was by reading it in the newspapers, which said the services were private. I didn't attend the funeral because I interpreted private services to mean we weren't invited.

There's always been an ongoing connection between Burnett people, and yet nobody ever called or said anything to Al and me about going. Later on, we heard through the grapevine that Carol was upset with us for missing the funeral. As much as he had hurt her, she was upset when he passed away.

So were we. We should have been there to pay our last respects to a man who figured so prominently in our lives. When we did find out, we called Carol but couldn't get through to her, so we left an apology with her assistant.

I wish somebody new would come into her life—that would certainly be nice. I believe women sometimes get hurt so badly they just don't want to deal with men anymore. It's just not worth it. Carol is a survivor, though, and a great lady, and my life has been all that much better for having had the privilege of being a part of hers.

Hosting "Win, Lose or Draw

Gamesmanship

Beginning in 1988, I hosted the daytime version of the game show *Win, Lose or Draw* for two years. This came about because Burt Reynolds is a huge charades fan and loves to play it after dinner with friends. As the story goes, he had Fred Astaire over to his house one night, and Burt insisted they play. Fred, however, wasn't very good at it. When it was his turn he got the title, "Charge of the Light Brigade." Fred, being the shy type to begin with, was at a loss, so Burt grabbed a chalk board and said, "Well, then just draw it if you can't act it out."

Fred drew eight zillion tiny little soldiers, and everybody got to laughing so hard that Burt started playing a version of charades in which people could *only* draw their clues.

One night a number of years later, Al and I were at Snuff Garrett's house, the producer of "The Night the Lights Went Out in Georgia," along with Burt, Sally Field, whom he was dating at the time, Trini Lopez, and his date. After dinner we all played this new game Burt was now calling Win, Lose or Draw.

I have to admit at first I thought it was the dumbest thing I'd ever seen in my life. However, everyone seemed to get a kick out of it. The game continued to prove such a hit at Burt's dinner parties that he and his good friend Bert Convy formed Burt and Bert Productions to try to sell it to TV.

Buena Vista Television, a division of Disney, bought it, and Bert Convy, who was already a popular actor and game show host, agreed to front the nighttime syndicated version. However, his contract precluded him from hosting it for daytime TV, so he and Burt Reynolds set about to find the perfect host for the daytime version. My agent called Al one day and ran the possibility of my doing it by him. Al said he thought it was a great idea. So did I, but I had my doubts it would ever happen. "Look," I told Al, "they're never going to hire a woman to host a game show."

Al disagreed, adding that it would give me a chance to be "myself" on camera. I went to the audition and found out Burt and Bert had already tried out a lot of stand-up comics without being able to find one they thought was right for the show. They were looking for something different than the typically glib game show host. Both Burt and Bert and Richard Kline, the executive producer of the show (not the actor—same name, different person), were incredibly supportive of me. NBC, however, remained on the fence. The Disney people too were a little bit leery of having a female host, but Burt, Bert, and Richard prevailed and I eventually got the job.

I became a member of a very select club, one of the few women who ever hosted a game show on American television. Several years earlier, Betty White had one that lasted only thirteen weeks, *For Men Only,* for which she won an Emmy. And actress Elaine Joyce hosted *The Dating Game* for a short while. It was a great job, of course, but it did make my schedule a little hectic. For the two years I hosted *Win, Lose or Draw,* I was also doing *Mama's Family.* I worked on the sitcom Monday through Friday, and then every other weekend I would shoot ten episodes of *Win, Lose or Draw.*

We always had two male celebrities and two female celebrities on the show, plus a male and female contestant, to make up equal teams of the women against the men. The show had no budget and I was forever fighting for bigger prizes. When we were first starting, if we got to the end of the game and there were two or three minutes left, Bert Convy, who was a much more hands-on producer than Burt Reynolds, and Richard would come to me and say, "Why don't you just go out on the edge of the stage and do questions and answers?" Mind you, we were back at CBS, shooting *once again* on the same stage 33 on which I'd done the Burnett show and the NBC version of *Mama's Family.* And once again someone wanted me to do what Carol had done all those years. I didn't want to do it! *This was a game show,* I kept telling them!

It was Al who came up with a great alternative. He suggested instead we have a supply of simple one-word puzzles, and call people from the audience to do them for a hundred bucks. I loved that.

Because I was a woman, hosting a game show meant I had to deal with things men in the same position never think twice about. For instance, I've never fought so hard in my life over wardrobe. When a male game show host is hired, he goes to someplace like Botany 500, they give him a bunch of butt-ugly suits, and he kind of mixes and matches. With a woman, I discovered, it's a whole different thing. You have hosiery, shoes, accessories, and jewelry to deal with, and you've got to look different every day, because women out there will absolutely bash your wardrobe if you don't. They'll bash it regardless. I guess it's something in our genes. They'll call or write in and say, "What the hell were you wearing last Thursday! Wednesday you looked great, but Thursday . . ."

I used my own wardrobe when I started, but dressing for five shows a week, it didn't take long to go through everything in my closet. Sometimes I would dress conservatively, sometimes I'd wear trendy stuff, but either way, the producers were forever changing their mind.

One of the biggest problems with the show (and show business in general) were those goddamned suits. Not the ones I had to wear, the ones who told me which ones I had to wear. Most of them have degrees from wonderful schools, but no on-the-job experience. They don't start in the mail room anymore and as a result only know what they read in books, or what their research shows them. They're used to running shows by computer rather than their imaginations.

I'd come to the show in a dress and they'd say they didn't like the way it looked. I'd come the next week in leather pants and red sweater and they'd say, *this* is a great look on you, *this* is the way you need to be dressed.

Fine, until Arleen Sorkin, the soap opera actress, came on the show one day. She showed up in a miniskirt with a little hat on, and the suits went crazy! "Wouldn't it be fun if you kind of dressed like that," they said. So the following week I wore my short leather skirt and they said, "Yeah, that's a great look," until they decided I should be more conservative again. So it was back to the dresses and slacks, back and forth, back and forth, until they finally hired some wardrobe consultants who decided to dress me in suits, scarves, and pearl earrings. I wound up looking more like "News Break from Washington." I argued with them forever that I was supposed to be in a living room playing a very casual game. The guest stars, meanwhile, kept showing up in everything from Levi's to sweats, not to mention Richard Simmons, who would come in his Dolphin shorts, while I looked like Leslie Stahl, right down to the pearls around my neck.

These "experts" said they'd done lots of research which told them that what women *really* want to see in the morning, when we were on, was a man they'd like to *sleep with!* Hey, guys, I told them, that wasn't my job! Besides, I was a woman, remember? Let the audience fantasize about Bert Convy!

Yes, they said, but if I wasn't dressed "strong," it would look as if I wasn't in control. One day I wore a really pretty blouse and a skirt that they agreed looked great on me, except it didn't make me appear to be in control. What I couldn't get them to understand was that we were successful, why screw with it? Let's face it. I do not have Vanna White's body, and it isn't that easy to make me look "adorable" while maintaining that control they were so desperate for me to have. Finally, Richard actually began picking out the outfits I was to wear, with a list of what went with what.

I remember one day I was in my dressing room and my wardrobe assistant, Trudy Otterson, was helping me get into this red suit, which didn't fit me at all, and we both started crying from laughing so hard. We finally gave up and went on to the next outfit.

Well, Richard was expecting me to be in that red suit. When I returned to my dressing room after the show, Trudy was shaking so badly getting me dressed she was putting stuff on me upside down. "What is the matter with you," I finally asked.

"Richard came in and screamed at me," she said. "He warned me, 'Don't you ever vary from the wardrobe list.'" He had reamed her out and cursed her to the heavens, which he was prone to do.

I told Trudy I'd take care of it and went out to see Richard. When I found him, I said, "Don't you ever, *ever* raise your voice at someone who is working for me. Trudy does not work for you. She's here to help me get dressed."

He said, "I'm having a little problem with you. I need you to be paying more attention to camera one, and talking to those people—"

"Did you just hear what I said to you?" Now, screaming was a natural state for Richard. He used to curse and scream so loud in the booth you could hear it coming through the cameramen's headsets. That's the way he liked to direct, and that's the way he liked to confront people.

"YES, BUT YOU'RE NOT PAYING ANY ATTENTION TO CAMERA ONE—"

"WHAT I WEAR IS MY BUSINESS AND DON'T YOU EVER SCREAM AT TRUDY AGAIN, DO YOU UNDERSTAND ME?"

"IF I DON'T SCREAM AT TRUDY WILL YOU LOOK AT CAMERA ONE?"

"FINE!"

"FINE!"

It was one of the very few times up until then I had actually stood up for myself in this business, and I was damn proud of it. The thing that struck me about screaming back at Richard was that once I did it, he had a new respect for me. "Okay," he must have thought, "this broad has balls!"

Still, the battle raged on in one form or another. I almost quit one time when Richard and one of the Disney dudes walked into my room while I was dressing. "Oh, we forgot. We thought it was Bert Convy today." Yeah, right. They did this often, always unannounced, usually while I'd be putting my pantyhose on. Finally, I told Al about it. He called Richard and told him how it was going to be from now on.

"Let me tell you something, Richard," he said.

"What's that, Al?"

"Rule number one, you don't ever walk into Vicki's room while she's getting dressed. If you do, I'm going to break your knees."

"You're going to break my knees? Is that a threat?"

"No," Al said, "that's a promise."

Once more, I learned that Al was the one person who protected me. There was no agent, manager, or any one of the so-called handlers in this business who would have fought so hard for me against the suits. Richard kept his knees, Al held his temper, and I retained my sanity.

Another time I got sick and Richard decided to replace me without getting my approval or even asking me what I thought.

When the star of a show becomes ill, the producers don't arbitrarily replace him or her. That's what companies have insurance for. If a day is lost, taping is rescheduled. Generally, unless it's a live show, tapings are done far enough in advance so that missing a day isn't a catastrophe. When I asked why I couldn't have a day to allow my 103 degree temperature to subside, Richard Kline said, "Sally Struthers is coming in to take your place. She'll be good."

I really like Sally, but when I saw the show with her waving into the camera, smiling and saying, "Get well, Vicki, we miss you," I got really angry. I said to Al, "If they want to replace me, why don't they just do it for good?"

Again, it was Al who fought for me. He called and this time said, "There is no reason to replace Vicki because she's sick. You wouldn't do this to Bert Convy. If you want a new hostess, you can get yourself one."

Richard screamed into the phone at the top of his lungs. *"LET ME UNDERSTAND THIS. ARE YOU TELLING ME THAT VICKI IS WALKING OUT OF HER CONTRACT?"*

Al said, "You're goddamn right."

"I'll call you back when I calm down."

Five minutes later the phone rang. It was Richard again, and he hadn't exactly calmed down. *"LET ME UNDERSTAND THIS. ARE YOU TELLING ME . . ."*

When their conversation, such as it was, ended, I called Bert Convy myself. "Please don't tell Burt Reynolds," he said. "He'll fly in and hit somebody. I'll come over and take care of this."

After that, Richard Kline was a perfect gentleman. Never raised his voice to me again.

Burt and Bert were without doubt the two most gorgeous bosses I ever had, and among the most thoughtful as well. They always saw to it that enormous flower arrangements followed me everywhere I went, there were limousines, and massive amounts of food in the dressing rooms.

In 1988, my very first year as a game show host, I was nominated for an Emmy for *Win, Lose or Draw*. When I got to the hotel for the ceremonies there were flowers everywhere. It looked like the Kentucky Derby. I couldn't even get them home and wound up having to leave them behind. Bob Barker won, but I had more flowers.

*E*arly in the show's run we had Cesar Romero on. All I knew of Cesar Romero at the time were the movies he'd made that I'd seen when I was growing up. He came on the show, walked up to the board, and said to me, "I have loved you for years."

Cesar Romero? *Dip me, you fool!*

It dawned on me then that if you're around long enough in this business, everybody knows you. They've either grown up watching you or they've worked with you, or they're legends sitting at home watching television like the rest of us. You never know who is on the other side of that camera watching you. I wouldn't have guessed in a million years that Cesar Romero even knew who I was. *But he did.*

Win, Lose or Draw taught me firsthand how hard it is to be a game show host. There's a lot going on at the same time, and it's the host's job to manage it all. You've got to keep the game moving, keep track of the score, segue in and out of commercials, get the thing played by the end of the half hour. On top of that, *Win, Lose or Draw* was meant to give the audience the impression they were in someone's living room. So I had to schmooze with the guests, do a little laughing and cutting up, and still get the game in. I felt as if I'd gotten a crash course in "Dick Clark." The best game show hosts make it all look so easy.

This was the first time I really felt comfortable being on camera as myself. Up until this time, I'd always hidden behind characters. The show helped me to discover I had a nice rapport with the other celebrities, and that they were comfortable with me.

Among our most devoted fans were students. I used to get invited by college campuses all the time to come and do *Win, Lose or Draw* contests. We were being talked about and written up constantly. And then, at the height of our popularity, we were abruptly canceled.

In spite of the fact that he was a total maniac, Richard Kline became a good friend of mine. He phoned me at home one day absolutely furious because NBC had called Disney and said they wanted to pick us up for another thirteen weeks. Disney said either pick us up for a full year or not at all. NBC said, no, thirteen weeks, the normal pickup cycle, was their limit. Disney stood firm, and NBC passed. Suddenly, we were dead in the water. Richard was so upset because he hadn't even been consulted by Disney. Nor were Burt and Bert. Disney just made this blanket all-or-nothing decision, and let the show die. By all rights they should have agreed to the thirteen weeks—if that's what you're offered, then that's what you take—and we would have stayed on. The result of all this was, we were canceled while still a hit.

*I*t was during *Win, Lose or Draw* that I decided to change my name. One day, the actress Dee Wallace Stone was our guest. She told a lovely story about how when she married Christopher Stone, and because it was Christmas and they didn't have a ton of money, she wanted to do something for her new husband, so she added his name to hers. That struck me as so sweet, and so romantic, I thought I would do the same thing for Al. So on Father's Day, 1988, I legally added Schultz to my last name and became Vicki Lawrence Schultz.

Courtney thought this was great, because she was sick of being asked if Steve Lawrence was her father. For everyone else, however, me included, it turned out to be the biggest pain in the ass. To begin with, the paperwork was just unbelievable. It makes you wonder how anything gets done in government at all. Trying to get Social Security to change my ID, getting union cards amended, then having them tell you your name is too long, there's not enough room on their computers, did I want Vicki Lawrence S., no, I'd prefer Vicki L. Schultz, thank you.

I went to all that trouble, then decided to surprise Al by giving him my new name all wrapped up in a box like a little gift. When he opened it, his first reaction was, "Well, this is really sweet, honey, but, Vicki Lawrence *Schultz?*"

I told him about Dee Wallace Stone and he said, "That's a lovely name. But Vicki Lawrence *Schultz?*"

As it turned out, nobody could ever get it right. I became Vicki Lawrence *Short,* or Vicki Lawrence *Schwartz.* Before, when *Win, Lose or Draw*'s announcer, Bob Hilton, would introduce me, it was always, "Here's your hostess,

Vicki Lawrence!" Now it became the hardest thing for him to say. "Here's your hostess, Vicki Lawrence *SSCCHH-UULLTTZZZ . . .!*" It never sounded . . . *right.*

I kept my new name for about a year and a half before I finally said the hell with it, people are having too much trouble dealing with it, including me. Al agreed. He said you're Vicki Lawrence and that's the end of it.

Still, a lot of my fans and most people who know me away from show business know me now as Mrs. Schultz.

Or Mrs. Schwartz.

I think I always loved the ocean but didn't realize how much until I met Al. On one of our very first dates he took me sailing. Ever since we've been married, we've always had a boat. We used to keep ours at Marina Del Rey, which meant we spent an hour and a half on the freeways each way every weekend just to get to it. *If* we could get to it, which because of traffic sometimes became just impossible.

Every summer we would come down to Long Beach, about forty miles south of Los Angeles, for a great week of yacht racing. We'd bring the boat down to the yacht club in June, stay at the Clarion for Race Week, stroll around Naples, and always make a point of walking along the canals. The more we explored the area the more we loved it. We used to fantasize about buying this house across from the yacht club painted just like our house in the valley, yellow with white trim, and living on the water.

Then, in the fall of 1985, we decided if we were ever going to actually do it, the time was now, before the kids were at an age where they'd hate us for moving them away from their schools and friends.

Part of our motivation was wanting to leave Hidden Hills. Everything we had loved about the area had turned *nouveau riche.* Everything now came down to who's got the most money, who can build the biggest house, and of course, let's not forget the quickly escalating war between the tennis people and the horse people.

When we first moved to Hidden Hills it was so rural and so charming. The young girl who first taught Courtney to horseback-ride had this family of ducks that would cross the road every morning to the creek across the way, and every afternoon Mrs. Ducky and her babies would cross back again. By the time we moved away, the residents were petitioning to get the ducks off the road so they could get home faster at night.

That's when I said to myself, isn't this why we moved here in the first place? To watch ducks cross the road, to have our kids ride horses?

There was more. Al used to work out with a sheriff in the Valley who was stationed in Malibu Canyon. He served both the Valley and Malibu. About the time we decided to leave, there was a lot of drug and crime trouble starting with the young people. One day the Sheriff said to Al, "I would much rather go to the beach and bust surfers than I ever would want to deal with teenagers in the Valley. You go down to the beach, they've been surfing all day, they're doing a little grass, they're mellowed out, and when you bust them they go, 'Hey man, that's cool.' Back in the valley, the kids are doing booze and coke, and are mean."

Also, our kids were getting to the age where they were starting to socialize. Living in Hidden Hills meant if they wanted to go to the movies one of us had to drive them down to Ventura Boulevard. If they wanted to go to a party one of us had to drive them. If they wanted to go bowling . . . you get the idea.

Still, it wasn't an easy move to make. That day in November 1986, when the realtor came, Courtney said, "What is he doing here?" I had to tell her then that we'd sold our house and bought one in Long Beach. She went running out the door and wouldn't speak to us for a long time. It was almost a year before she really liked us again.

The house we bought in Long Beach had been empty for five years because the little den area in front had suffered a lot of water damage. The roof was no good, so every time it rained the place flooded. News travels fast in a neighborhood, and the house was marked. Still, I decided to give it a look.

The realtor took me over, I walked in, and the first thing I discovered was this little area with a small door next to the entrance. I asked the realtor if it was a closet, he opened it with a flourish and said proudly, "It's an elevator."

I said, "I'm sorry, I can't deal with an elevator in my home." I had visions of Garrett holding secret meetings in the shaft and me accidentally killing him.

Finding something spacious on Naples Island is not easy. A year later, I took another look at the house with the elevator, because it had three stories and by far the best layout of anything we'd looked at. We decided to buy it.

Our movers took one look at it and were ready to leave, until they found out it had an elevator. They got out of their truck, stood on the street, looked up at the three stories of the house and said, "You've got to be kidding."

The elevator, by the way, worked out great. It turned out to be a real lifesaver, because the kitchen is on the second floor. If you have eight zillion bags of groceries, or a ton of dry cleaning, or if you're going on a trip, you don't have to schlep everything up and down the stairs.

As I said, Courtney didn't speak to us for about a year. The move happened when she was twelve years old and starting junior high school. She'd sit in the dark on the sofa. If I asked her what she was doing she'd say, "Nothing."

"It's a beautiful day."

"Yes."

"Don't you think you should go out?"

"No."

Now, though, when she goes back to visit her friends in the Valley, she can't believe how lucky she is to be down here. There's so much to do for her, water-skiing, jet-skiing, boating. Garrett was fine with the move. He immediately became the leader of the new neighborhood.

I had often talked about how nice it would be to own some real art, so in 1993, for our nineteenth anniversary, we decided we would start buying one piece of quality art a year.

We began looking in Laguna, searching for some exciting discovery, which we didn't find. Nothing really leapt out at us. On the way back, we realized that the inspiration to buy art had to happen when it happened, and when it did, that would be our anniversary gift to each other.

We were driving back through Newport Beach when we passed this great old nautical antique store on Pacific Coast Highway. I told Al I'd always wanted to go in it, and as we were in the middle of redecorating our house with a nautical theme, we decided to check it out.

I anticipated a lot of ship's bells and lanterns, but in the window there was this wonderful painting, a turn-of-the-century oil, of a China trader. "Now, that's what I want for my anniversary, honey," I told Al.

We walked in and discovered two rooms in the back filled with nothing but antique, collectible sea oils. We stayed there for more than three hours and received quite an education from the proprietor. We now have our first oil hanging over the mantel. Of course, our redecorating budget got shot to hell, but we do love staring at that old ship.

Al was more reluctant to buy an old oil than I was, but there's something so romantic about them to me. I know the artists I covet, Montague Dawson, Charles Patterson, and, of course, James Buttersworth. They are all similar in style, but each is striking in his own way.

When I asked Al if he loved it as much as I did, he said, "Yeah, but I hope you don't just love ocean stuff because I do."

"No," I said, "the ocean is very peaceful to me." I was reminded then of something a psychic once told me. "You are an Aries," she said. "Your brain and your guts are in Aries, but your heart and your soul are in Pisces." Al is a Pisces, which means we're soul mates. So guess what, Al, you're stuck with me.

Such is life in Paradise.

With Lily Tomlin.

Games—Televised and Otherwise

By 1990, both *Win* and *Mama's Family* had ended their runs. I began looking for another sitcom and wasn't having much success. It was the same old problem. Everyone at the networks wanted me to play a mother, which I really didn't want to do again. As a result, I found myself sitting home unemployed and depressed.

Then early one Sunday in 1991 I got a call at home from my agent, Tony Fantozzi. "Guess where I just went for breakfast," he said.

"I don't know, Tony."

"I went to the deli in Malibu. Guess who was there?"

"I don't know, Tony."

"Fred Silverman. Guess what Fred said to me."

"I don't know, Tony."

"Fred said that Brandon Tartikoff wants him to get into the sitcom business. But 'It don't matter how good you are, if you ain't got the right star, you can't do a hit sitcom.' Then I said to Fred, 'What about Vicki Lawrence?' and what do you think Fred said to me?"

"I don't know, Tony."

" 'Sit down!' "

"No!"

"Yes. We had a nice long talk and what I want you to do is, in your nicest handwriting, write Fred a letter telling him why it is you want to do a sitcom, some of the ideas you have, get it done and messenger it to him today."

I wrote the letter, and the next thing I knew, I had a meeting set for Tuesday morning at NBC with Tony Fantozzi, Brandon Tartikoff, and Fred Silverman.

There was a good feeling between all of us as we tossed out ideas. It didn't take us very long to agree on one of the ideas, a sitcom with me as an undercover cop—*I Love Lucy* meets *Barney Miller*—and to decide how to go forward. This was a clear lesson to me. I realized Fred Silverman was the type of power producer needed to open the networks' endless sets of closed doors. Suddenly, I felt like Cinderella in television heaven, where the clock always stops at 11:59.

I *adored* Fred Silverman. He wanted to do our show the way they were done in the old days. For one thing, he actually asked me who I'd like to have as my leading man. We came up with Dan Hedaya, a very funny actor. Next, he asked who I wanted as my nutty neighbor. I said I would love to work with Dorothy Lyman again. Who would I like for the sergeant? I said Roger Mosley from *Magnum, P.I.* My silly boss? Max Wright, from *Alf.*

The only problem we had turned into a major one. We could only use "network-approved" writers. Fine, except in my opinion, the "network-approved" writers didn't know how to write character-driven comedy. Their script was really nothing more than a series of bad "jokes."

It was too bad, because we had had the nucleus for something really special. Fred had put together this incredible cast for me, and he had the muscle to get us on the air. However, I knew that it would take good writing to keep us there.

I ended up trying to write some of it myself. Fred would call me at home six o'clock in the morning, saying we had to fix such and such a scene. I'd say I wasn't really a scriptwriter and he'd say it didn't matter because I knew the character better than anyone.

During all of this, Brandon Tartikoff was very high on us, saying the show would be his final gift to NBC. He was, at the time, in the process of handing over the reins of the network to Warren Littlefield. As you may have heard, it was not the friendliest of transitions.

At run-throughs, Tartikoff and Littlefield would sit at opposite ends of the studio without looking or speaking to each other. After, we'd all go into a room for something I laughingly referred to as "network notes." Warren would say he thought this should happen and we should change that scene, after which Brandon would say something like, "We're not doing Dostoyevsky here." I tried to stay out of the line of fire.

Looking back, perhaps it's not all that surprising in spite of all our good intentions and Fred's muscle power that the pilot wasn't picked up. Still, I was devastated.

In the meantime, Al was convinced I might be better off as a TV "personality," rather than doing yet another sitcom character. All during the time I worked on Silverman's pilot, Al had kept hammering away at the idea of my doing a talk show. He'd gotten the idea during the run of *Win, Lose or Draw*. One day after a taping he turned to me and said, "You know you're really good at this." So, while I was trying to get the sitcom to go, Fantozzi hooked Al up with David Fein and John Goldhammer, two executive producers who were interested in the possibility of my doing a talk show with them.

Fein and Goldhammer had tried and failed to launch a talk show the year before. Fantozzi had decided to put them together with Al, just prior to the annual National Association of Television Program Executives (NATPE) convention, in Miami, where every cable and syndicated TV show is first sold.

Al suggested that Fein and Goldhammer ask around at the convention if anyone might be interested in a talk show starring Vicki Lawrence. The first syndicator they met with was Westinghouse/Group W, who said they were very interested. Westinghouse hadn't created a hit show in a while and was eager to get back into the game.

Meanwhile, I continued to suffer a heavy dose of performer's paranoia, as in, I'll never work again. It was a difficult, stressful time, and Al and I were at each other's throats. I was unemployed and panicked about finances. Courtney was about to start Stanford. Al began talking about going back to work as a makeup artist because the windfall that Carol and Joe had predicted would come from doing *Mama* hadn't as yet materialized.

To pass the time, I began riding a Lifecycle and watching daytime TV. I watched all the talk shows for weeks, and determined there were a number of things missing from them for me as a viewer. After a week I began to feel I must be the last normal person on the planet. Where did they get these people and why did they deserve so much air time? The other thing that bothered me was that America had lost its sense of humor. From the looks of things, we had forgotten how to laugh about our everyday predicaments.

A week after NATPE, I had my first meeting with Group W's president, Derk Zimmerman. It was a Friday evening, Al arranged for a limo, and I went by myself. He said, "You'll be fine. You know what you're talking about. You don't need a husband tagging along." I arrived at Derk's office about a half hour before the meeting and was waiting in the lobby when, the next thing I know, Derk came walking out of his office, saw me and said, "You're here already? Well, come on back."

We talked for a half hour before anyone else arrived. I had never laid eyes on Mark Itken, the William Morris agent who was going to package the show. When he came in, he kissed me on the cheek and whispered in my ear, "Pretend you know me."

Fein and Goldhammer arrived shortly thereafter, and I noticed both were glaring at me, as in, how dare I have begun the meeting without them? This in spite of the fact that Derk and I had gotten along famously that first half hour; so much so that by the time the meeting officially started he was ready to roll tape. "I like this woman," he announced to the others, "so let's go."

So we went. The first stop was San Francisco that June for what Derk called a "wet" test (I guess as opposed to a dry run). We did five shows, one a day, on the borrowed news set of KPIX, a Group W station. After one of the shows that Al and I felt could have gone much more smoothly, Derk said, "Al, who cares? The important thing is she can talk. Even more important, she can listen. That's all I need to know." Hallelujah! I had passed my wet test (actually, it all sounded a little kinky to me)!

It took another year to get the show on the air, during which Fein and Goldhammer decided to move on. Meanwhile, I continued to study the other talk shows, and one day I said to Al, "Our show is going to have to be different." If a producer were to come to me and say tomorrow we're doing "men who've raped their daughters and now they're raising the kids together," my reaction would be to slap the shit out of the men, rush the women to a good doctor, take all the babies and run. That phrase became my battle cry even before we went on the air. I wanted

187

our show to be fun. Life is much too serious to be taken seriously. That's my motto and that's the spirit with which I put my show together.

I also wanted celebrities. There are a lot of stars who won't do daytime because of what it has become. They don't want to be bashed. In the beginning, we had to fight really hard for the few celebrities we were able to get.

As far as doing "serious" shows, they had to be issues I cared about, like censorship, education, health care, the environment, raising teenagers. Worthwhile topics. Plastic surgery, yes. Sex change, no. I can't get into "transvestites and the women they live with." Somewhere the line had to be drawn. On one side, Vicki. On the other, Geraldo.

We debuted August 31, 1992, and were instantly well received by both the critics and the public. *The Hollywood Reporter,* an influential trade publication, wrote a love letter to us disguised as a review, written by Rick Sherwood, which included the following:

> It could be the talk show of the '90's—a more sincere, more polite and less sensational look at people, celebrities and lifestyle. . . .
>
> Vicki Lawrence, long known for her comedic talents on "The Carol Burnett Show" and "Mama's Family," has been able to adapt her winning personality to the demands of the talk show circuit with a mellowed, more mature approach that still keeps a watch on the comedic buzzer. . . .
>
> Lawrence succeeds where others have failed because she plays fan and interviewer, a kind of anywoman asking the questions fans might ask. . . . Everything about this show is fun and fancy-free, and if I'm reading things right, it's the way of the 1990's.

We started with 136 stations, and reached 192 at our peak. The schedule was grueling, the hardest I'd ever worked, as well as the most chaotic. We taped twenty-four shows a month, two a day, three days a week.

Monday was our really big meeting, where we talked about how the shows would turn out in our dreams. There were times when everything fell through, we didn't have a show for Thursday night and had to quickly throw one together.

Also on Mondays, I'd do wardrobe and meet with my one and only writer, Monty Aidem, who always began those meetings by reminding me that Jay Leno has twenty writers and isn't half as funny, and that he, Monty, wasn't making much money. *Then* we'd talk about intros, outros, openings, and my personal take on each show.

Because we taped at the NBC studios in Burbank, a lot of people thought we were on the network. Actually, we were syndicated, and only about a third of our affiliates were NBC.

We happened to share a common hall with *The Tonight Show.* When we first started production, Jay's people put tape down the hall. Their attitude was, *don't cross this line!* They must have thought we were just another stupid little daytime talk show. We had a common makeup room where we all went to get made up and have our hair done. If anyone from our show happened to schmooze with any of their guests, they would send someone over to our offices to remind us not to "bother" them.

Things began to lighten up when they realized we were there to stay. One day, Al put a note on the ladies' room door that said, "This bathroom is for use by *The Tonight Show* staff from three to five PM only. The rest of the time it is strictly for *Vicki!* personnel." He caught the executive producer of *The Tonight Show*, Debbie Vickers, staring at it intently. He walked up to her and said, "Debbie, *it's a joke!*"

The one person from *The Tonight Show* who had always been supportive of me from the very get-go was Fred De Cordova. One day he came up, put his arm around me and said, "You're so adorable. Too bad you don't screw around."

"Oh, I don't know," I said. "For you, Fred, I might make an exception."

*M*y dressing room wasn't huge, especially when you consider half the time I had other people in there. A larger one was available upstairs, but I opted to be close to the stage, so I could hear what was going on in the hall. I just thought it was better if, say, Lily Tomlin was on the show, for me to be able to hear her voice, come out, and say hi.

By the way, when Lily did the show, I did exactly that, went next door and said hi. A half hour later we were such fast friends my stage manager knocked on the door and said, "No kidding, ladies, we've got a show to do." She brought all her scrapbooks with her. We always asked the guests to bring us some pictures, or some clips. Well, God love her, she dismantled her whole life for me! She had her first photo composite from New York, and her old autograph book. She had Tony Curtis's autograph! I told her that when I was young, I wrote letters from stars to me and mailed them to myself, then took them to school and showed them to everyone. "My God," she said. "We were so much alike! I used to do that all the time."

I wrote one to myself from Debbie Reynolds that went something like, "Dear Vicki, When I got back from Hawaii, I told Eddie all about our trip." I would have written her back, but just couldn't find the time.

Anyway, my dressing room was connected to a mirror image of itself, with one of those tacky little sliding doors in the middle, like a train compartment, that locks with nothing more than a fingerlatch, which didn't work too well. It became pretty much of a ritual that every time I got dressed for the show, Dina, my dresser, would hand me my pantyhose. No one ever said that rituals had to make sense. I always faced Dina while I put them on, so I wouldn't have to stick my butt in her face. This is one of the little intricacies of show business you'll only get here, friends.

One day, Esther Williams was a guest on the show and happened to be on the other side of the door. Without warning she slid it open. When she saw me she smiled and said, "Oh, sweetie, here you are! Meet my puppy . . ." Thank God I wasn't doing anything more embarrassing than watching Rush Limbaugh on the TV.

It became a running gag between Dina and me that the most hideous thing was going to happen, that one day we wouldn't be so lucky as we were with Esther, and that somebody would open that sliding door and be greeted by my butt. Sure enough, we were doing a "classic sitcom reunion" show and one of our guests was Pat Harrington, who had played Schneider on *One Day at a Time*. Pat had done a couple of *Win, Lose or Draw*s with me, and I found him to be a very funny guy.

So there I was, putting on my pantyhose, and that sliding door flew open. Pat took one look, yelled *"Shit!"* at the top of his lungs, and slammed the door. There was an embarrassing pause, after which came a polite little knock. "You look great, Vicki!"

When you invest so much time in your career, you look for help wherever you can find it. Being eighteen and trying to juggle school and *The Carol Burnett Show* was one thing, having a career and trying to raise two kids was quite another. Every so often, my mom would volunteer to help out, which was great, except mother could never deal with my kids.

One time when Al and I were living in Malibu, as a favor she volunteered to take them for the weekend. I said, wow, nice treat, although I was a little reluctant to send the kids to her house because mother was always saying to us when we were growing up that she wanted a son. I really believed she was so jealous I had one, she might actually hurt Garrett.

But I sent the kids over, and Al and I planned a romantic weekend, which lasted all of three hours. That's when the phone rang. It was mother, saying the kids had colds and she just didn't know what to do about it, so she was bringing them back.

As they've grown, I see them differently than I did when they were babies. Back then, by comparison, their little colds seemed so simple. They're teenagers now, and in case you didn't know it, let me clue you in: teenagers are brilliant! It's amazing, when your kids hit thirteen you suddenly turn into a moron. You can't believe you've lived on the earth as long as you have, as stupid as you are.

Of course, geniuses aren't always such great students. Two Christmases ago, Garrett pulled a D on his history final. His class got their test grades back on the last day of school before Christmas, which is not a serious day. They were sitting around eating candy and watching *It's a Wonderful Life*.

Now, I have a 1941 Wurlitzer juke box in our den, the first piece of furniture Al ever bought for our house when we started living together. He found it in the back of an antique store and I love it. It's got all my parents' old 78s in it. One of my favorites is Bing Crosby's "White Christmas."

When Garrett was thirteen, several years after we moved to Long Beach, I wanted to enroll him in Cotillion. He went one time and thought it was the biggest crock he'd ever seen. Girls wearing little white gloves, boys taking them cups of punch, he wanted nothing to do with it.

I could understand, even empathize with him. My mom did the same thing to me. When I was in sixth grade I had to take ballroom dancing lessons. I was the tallest girl in my class, so when I'd dance with the guys in class, their faces would be in my chest.

Still, I thought the experience was worthwhile. "Wouldn't it be nice if you knew how to waltz on your wedding night?" I asked him. So, periodically, we have dancing lessons using the records on the juke box for accompaniment. Because I love it so, I often play "White Christmas."

Back at school, he went up to the teacher and asked if there was anything he could do to get the D off his record. His teacher thought about it and said, "I'll tell you what, Garrett. You stand up in front of all these boys here and sing 'White Christmas' and I'll let you off the hook."

When he came home that day, he told me the story and said, "Mom, you would have been so proud of me. Without even missing a beat, I stood in front of all those boys and did a perfect rendition of Bing Crosby doing 'White Christmas' . . . 'I'm . . . dreeeeeming . . . of a whiiiiite . . . Christmas . . .' "

The teacher was so impressed he bumped him up to a C.

I was beaming. "You see," I told him, "those dancing lessons are important!" Little smart-ass!

*G*arrett is really a great guy, even if he isn't always so forthcoming with his problems. What genius is? On the other hand, Courtney and I have an amazingly open relationship. Sometimes I hate it, because she'll tell me more than I ever wanted to know! It's really hard, I have to bite my lip and think to myself, oh God, I don't want to hear this!

193

When the Burnett show was running, and our hands were totally too full for us to watch our children, who were just babies really, we hired a housekeeper, Martha Krebs, a lovely German lady.

Before we hired her, I'd interviewed several others and had come up empty. Finally, I decided to place an ad in the papers. One night this nice lady called, I spoke to her, thought she sounded perfect, and insisted Al go interview her. When he got back he stormed into the kitchen. "For chrissake, Vicki, she was standing on a corner, had no teeth in front, and looked like a bag lady. I'll take over." That's when he found Martha.

And she was just great. Garrett was still in diapers, and one of her first days she had him on the little daybed in the kitchen, changing him, when Courtney asked if she could help. "Yes," Martha said, and Courtney pulled out a Pamper from the box. She then handed it to Martha and pointed to Garrett's little penis. "You see that there?" she asked.

"Yes?"

"You push that button and juice comes out!"

Out of the mouths of babes . . .

We've always been much more open about sex in my home than my parents were in theirs. I think it's better that way. For instance, when Courtney was five years old, she came home from school one day and wanted to know what the F word was. I wasn't ready for that one. We were living next door to my pediatrician, Bob Millhouse, a very good friend. I brought over a bottle of wine to his place and asked how I tell my five-year-old what the F word means.

He invited me in, opened the bottle, poured each of us a glass, and shared his wisdom with me. The most important thing, he said, was to talk about it. If I didn't, he warned, she would get it off the street. The reason kids don't talk to their parents about sex is because they know their parents can't deal with it. "Just flat out tell her," he said.

"Tell her what?"

"That it's an ugly word for a beautiful thing."

"But when you're five," I said, "it's not a beautiful thing."

"You're right, you're right . . . let's have another glass of wine and think about this . . ."

We talked it all out, until I felt fully prepared for my conversation with Courtney. I picked her up from school the next day and when we got home, I said, "Sit down, Courtney, I want to talk to you about what the F word means."

"Oh, I know what it means, mom. Anyway, I had a really good day at school . . ."

It turned out just as Bob predicted. All she wanted was to know that I *could* talk about it. Ever since, she tends to tell me more than I want to know, and we've had some pretty incredible conversations.

When Courtney was twelve, we were walking the dog one day, and she asked me about oral sex. She'd heard there was such a thing, and wanted to know what it meant. Some of the girls in her class had said that's where they drew the line. I said to myself, *that's where they draw the line?* I have to admit, I got in over my head that night (no pun intended). I racked my brain to come up with something. Courtney said, "You're not going to talk to me about this, are you?"

"Yes I am. I just need some time to formulate my thoughts." We got back, made the guys dessert, during which I kept on trying to figure out how to explain oral sex to someone still looking forward to her first kiss.

I have no idea what I said. I finally went to bed around two in the morning, and, surprise surprise, couldn't drop off. At one point Al asked if something was on my mind he could help me with. I just turned to him and said, "Don't ask. *Just don't ask!*"

When we were living in Hidden Hills the second time, before we moved to Long Beach, I decided, as I think every mother does, that the one thing my urban children were missing the most was experiencing "the whole life process." So we decided to let our cat, Sophie, get knocked up. Sophie had been Garrett's Christmas present in 1985, when he was eight years old. I had put a little note under the Christmas tree, saying this was a gift from Santa, and Garrett had to follow the ribbon through every single room, around every door, outside the house, all the way around. It finally ended up tied to a doorknob on the service porch. There sat Sophie.

We deliberately didn't have her fixed, to let her, and us, go through the experience of one litter. And that's just what it was—an experience. I know there are too many cats and how hard it is to get rid of the babies, which is why if I ever have the urge again to bring the farm to our home, we'll look at pictures.

Still, it was a wonderful night, and we all got to discuss the entire process of childbirth, what you have to go through, how it happens, all of it.

Al was sitting on the sofa talking on the phone, when Sophie jumped up next to him and rolled down into the crack between the cushions. Because she was so big and pregnant she couldn't get out. Al reached over to try and help her, when he suddenly cried out, "Vicki, her water's breaking!"

Isn't this wonderful! We all rushed Sophie into the spare bedroom. We closed it off entirely, got her a box, made her a little bed out of it, and proceeded with the Lamaze method of natural childbirth. We timed her little contractions and watched her back go up and her claws come out. She was in labor about an hour and a half. Because she was such a tiny cat, the vet had predicted she wouldn't have more than two kittens. After three, we congratulated her and closed the door to let her rest with what looked to us like little wet rats. The next morning, when we came in to see her, there were five adorable fluffy kittens, all cleaned up and happily nursing. *Way to go, Soph!*

She was such a neat cat. She used to go for walks with us, like a dog. When we moved to Long Beach, she became Miss Social. She ran around with everyone in the neighborhood and liked to sleep with a golden retriever down the street. One morning a neighbor of ours came up to our door crying. She told us that Sophie had been run over, was lying in the bushes and wouldn't let anyone touch her.

Al picked her up and we could plainly see that both her legs were badly broken. We rushed her to the veterinarian emergency room. The doctor put little wood splints on her and said she'd be fine. She walked around the house like Frankenstein for weeks. It would take her forever to climb into the litter box. We laughed so hard we cried. At the same time, of course, we felt so sorry for her. She stayed that way for a month, until we took her back to our vet, hoping to get the splints removed. The doctor took an X-ray and said nothing had healed because the bones weren't touching. The only alternative, he said, was to operate immediately.

He put steel pins in her legs and told us she had to be confined to prevent her from jumping until she healed. We cooped her up in our powder room and piled every piece of luggage we had on the toilet and sink so she couldn't jump. No one used the room for a month. One day, someone inadvertently left the door open and I caught sight of her going out the back. She jumped across to the neighbor's balcony and ran down the stairs.

I managed to grab her and immediately took her back to the vet. He examined her and said that the jump had broken one of the steel pins. He strongly suggested we put her to sleep. The kids were devastated, so I ruled that out immediately. He then suggested a specialist in Orange County who might be able to do something. By now we had named her the Six Million Dollar Cat!

We came home and recounted the whole story for Al, who suggested I call Betty White. "If she tells you to put Sophie to sleep, you can do it with a clear conscience, can't you?"

I said, "I guess I could." So I called Betty, told her the whole story, and asked her what she thought I should do. "Well, you know what I would do," she said. I waited to hear the worst. "I would take her to my emergency guy."

"Really?"

"Sweetie, you can't put a price on love."

"Yes, Betty!"

So I took Al's checkbook and went to see Dr. Rooks, the vet in Orange County, and he was fabulous! He used some plaster of Paris to build two little prostheses on the front of her legs, then nailed a bunch of little steel pins directly into her bones. That's when we started calling her Robocat.

This made her a little more mobile, but we still had to keep her cooped up for another eight weeks. When Dr. Rooks finally took the pins out and said, "Let her climb a tree," we all cried.

We took her back home and put her out in the park. She took one look at us, said, "I love you, goodbye." We hardly ever saw her again. We'd hear periodically from the people down the street with the golden retriever, where she slept, that she was okay. She'd come around occasionally when we walked our dogs, or when she wanted to be fed.

She hung out a lot at the yacht club. Al was down there one night having a cocktail, when Sophie came right across the top of the bar. Every guy there said, "Hi, Sophie, babe, how you doin'?"

It couldn't have been more than two or three months

after her leg had healed that someone found her dead in the street, run over by a car. Apparently, she was trying to come home from the Yacht Club and didn't quite make it. It was a sad day at the Schultz household. She was such a neat cat.

That left us with our two springer spaniels. Candy is a female black and white springer, so named for Candice Bergen. I brought her home one day from a pet store window. I was at the mall shopping and there she was. I couldn't stand it she was so adorable. I whimpered and cried for two days until Al said just go back and get the dog. So I did. I gave her to the kids, who were five and seven at the time, and asked them to give her a really sweet name. They came up with Candy.

We had Candy about a week and a half when I noticed Garrett running around the house calling her Candice Bergen. I asked him how he even knew who Candice Bergen was and he shrugged his shoulders. This was years before *Murphy Brown*. We were watching TV one night not long after, and on came Candice doing a perfume commercial. Well, there it was. And it could have been worse. We could have a dog named Bertice!

Al always had a male springer when he was a little boy, and wanted another one. So Max came about six months after Candy. I named him, because he just looked like a Max to me. When I got him, I put a little bow and a big old birthday card around his neck and shoved him into the living room. Surprise!

'*I*'ve never been a "girlfriend" person. I had a couple growing up, but I was never a hangout type with the girls. I never cared what color nail polish any of them wore, where they got that dress, or what kind of mascara they used. I'd rather have a beer with the guys.

However, I find as I get older there are a lot of things I have in common with women I didn't appreciate when I was younger. For instance, I think women *think* more about things than men do. I did a *Vicki!* show called "Why Can't a Man Be More Like a Woman?" We had John Gray on, author of *Men Are from Mars, Women Are from Venus,* Rita Rudner, who does a lot of war-between-the-sexes comedy, and a psychologist who said that when men are hurt, or something is wrong in their lives, they tend to hibernate, to go into their little caves. The problem is that women want to go into that cave with them, and talk to them, and don't understand that the reason the men are in that cave in the first place is that they don't want to be bothered. The one thing I did learn from that show was that when your husband is in the cave, accept that there's a DO NOT DISTURB sign up there. Leave them alone to sort it all out and they'll be back when they feel better. Of course, there are risks to all of this. As Rita Rudner pointed out, what if there's a blonde in the cave with them?

There's one in every crowd. Ritas, that is, not blondes.

I hope.

Right, Al?

Al? *AL?*"

Excuse me. I have to go now.

Mrs. Al and Mr. Vicki.

losing Credits

I tuned in to *Larry Sanders* last year for the first time. I knew it was on HBO but I could never figure out when or where. I have a bead on it now, which is good, because I plan on watching it every week from now on. I can absolutely identify with Larry Sanders.

The things that Larry (Garry Shandling) has to go through to get his show on the air are *exactly* the same types of things that I had to go through on mine. In one episode they brought a new head of late-night programming, and the first thing she said to Larry was, "Very frankly, your demos are down and therefore the revenues are down, so we need you to start doing your own live commercials." Larry reluctantly agreed to do a spot for the garden weasel. The only problem was, he couldn't get through it without making jokes, which infuriated the program executive.

It was basically the same situation on my show. Derk Zimmerman was forever crying about the breakdown of our ratings, that the demographic skew was all wrong. We'd go from too young to too old to too male. It seemed to change monthly. In the end, he decided we'd skewed too old and advertisers wanted younger viewers. Well, it is my humble opinion he doesn't know that the economic realities of America in the nineties are that you have to be over forty before you can afford to buy anything.

Then there was the question of my "being funny." It hadn't yet come to my doing commercials, but I did have constant battles with Group W over, how can I put this, me being the me they hired in the first place, the same me they kept complaining they didn't want to be as funny as . . . *me!* Get it? If you do, please write me a letter explaining it.

When I told my producer, Nancy Alspaugh, that Derk didn't want me to have a sense of humor, she said, "He just wants one he can control."

"Oh. In other words," I said, "he doesn't want a sense of humor, he wants to be a *censor* of humor."

*I*n January of 1994, as we approached the end of our second season, things heated up again between Group W and me. It all began the week after the Los Angeles earthquake, when Al and I went to Miami to attend the NATPE convention. We didn't know it at the time, but we were flying out of a natural disaster headlong into a man-made one.

When we got to Miami, we were met at the airport by Eduardo Santiago, our promotions manager, and as we were checking into our hotel, I turned to Al and said, "Hey, we did all right. This is a beautiful place."

The manager came over to greet us and said he had a lovely suite waiting for us upstairs. We decided to go to the bar and have a cocktail while our bags were brought up. When we finally got to the room, Al put the key in the door and couldn't open it. It wouldn't budge. Al had to give it a hard shoulder.

Once inside, we were greeted by a terrible odor, like from a dumpster outside a restaurant that's been filled a week too long. We finally pinned the source down to the refrigerator, which wasn't working properly. We closed it, unplugged it, and decided we wouldn't use the kitchen area at all.

We then went into the bedroom where, we discovered, the TV didn't work. I fiddled with the cable connection and when I got it just right the volume came on full blast. I figured if I stood in the same position for three days, I could watch TV. Al said, "That's okay, we don't really need a TV. Let's not stress over it, we're only going to be here for a few days."

"Fine," I said. "Let's go downstairs and get drunk enough so we can sleep here."

We went back to the bar, had a few cocktails, a little dinner. We had to be up by six to meet Eduardo and start making appearances on all the local radio stations. I put the little thing on the outside of the door, for breakfast, but forgot to mark the time, which ultimately didn't matter, since I later discovered they didn't start serving breakfast until seven.

The next morning, as we were getting dressed, Al called down to the manager to find out if there was any way to get coffee sent up and found out there wasn't. He then asked if there were any other suites available, and the manager, quite exasperated now, said, "Look, I'm up to my ears in VIPs here and do not have any other suites available. For your information, there's a coffeemaker in your kitchen!" With that, he hung up.

Al opened the dishwasher to look for it and out scrambled an army of cockroaches. Meanwhile, I started my shower, only to discover the drain wasn't working. Soon I was up to my ankles in soapy water. I got out, dried myself off and immediately stepped into my high heels, still stark naked, because I didn't want to step on one of the many cockroaches that *were* available before seven.

We got dressed and out of there, and were going down in the elevator along with three lovely ladies about my age, when one of them said, "My God, it's Vicki Lawrence! Are you staying here?"

"Yes . . ."

"Gee," one of the others said, "we would have thought you'd be getting the star treatment."

That's when I happened to look down and noticed we were riding in a Westinghouse elevator. "Oh my God," I said. "Everybody hold on!"

We finally got to the lobby, already ten minutes late, and found Eduardo pacing nervously back and forth. Just then the hotel manager came running up to me and said, "Miss Lawrence, we've had a few last-minute cancellations, and there's a better suite available on the eleventh floor, if you'd like to look at it . . ."

"Yes, please," I said, and turned to Eduardo and begged for three more minutes. Once upstairs, the assistant manager threw open the door to a lovely, immaculate blue and white suite. On the table was a big box of chocolates, a bottle of champagne, a beautiful floral arrangement, and a note that said, *"Welcome, Rolonda Watts."*

The next day, we went to Group W's assigned cubbyhole on the convention floor, where I was to greet station reps. Rich Sheingold, the head of Group W's sales, was also there, wearing what resembled a big snowshoe because he'd recently broken his foot. That afternoon, Derk told us Group W was throwing a big outdoor dinner party and wanted me to make a few remarks.

Okay, I thought to myself. I figured I'd prepare a couple of humorous comments. I got on the phone with my writer, Monty, and explained the situation to him. I thought we might do a Tonya Harding bodyguard joke, and maybe one about the two other shows Group W was trying to sell at the convention, *Jones and Jury* and something called *Truth or Tabloid*.

I also told Monty about the hell suite incident. He thought that had possibilities. I then went up to one of the salesmen and asked for the name of one of the buyers who was being difficult in negotiations so I could mention him in my speech.

The salesman thought it was a good idea, knowing people in any audience love hearing their name mentioned up on stage, and if anything, it would probably help make the sale. I took him aside and said, "When you get to the party tonight, you just eyeball someone who's being a pain, and I'll make a little joke about how they're sitting there enjoying the free food and the booze, and it's about time they got off the pot about the *Vicki* show." Nothing serious, just a little light humor.

That night, Eduardo, Al, and I took the limo to the party. When we arrived Eduardo asked me if I wanted something to drink. I said sure, how about a vodka tonic. Al wanted nothing, figuring correctly one of us needed to be on our toes. He became my designated husband for the remainder of the evening.

Eduardo checked back with me about an hour later to ask if I wanted another drink, which I declined. Only about an inch was gone from my glass. I had taken my cue from Al.

We were standing around schmoozing with some of the salesmen about how great things were going. The word was we already had 153 markets renewed, when Derk came over and announced it was time for everyone to take a seat.

Among those at our table were Derk, Rich, Bill Korn and his wife, and Lou Dennig, the director of programming for Blair Television, an organization that helps stations decide what shows to put on the air. At one point, to make conversation, I asked Lou what exactly it was that he did. Out of the corner of my eye I saw Derk look up in pure exasperation, as if to say, *God, she is the dumbest bitch that ever lived!*

Undaunted, I asked Lou if what he actually ran was a psychology booth. He smiled and said that buyers came to him when they were confused, and it was his job to unconfuse them about what would be best for their stations. He paused and then said, "You know where I first met you, Vicki?"

"No."

"I did the sound board in Traverse City, Michigan, when you did summer stock." I couldn't believe it! We started reminiscing about Traverse City and I could tell that, for reasons known only to him, Derk was really getting pissed off.

After salads, Derk stood up, made some opening remarks, then handed the mike over to me. I did the few little jokes that I prepared, including a very tame one about Tonya Harding—"You've all seen Rich limping around the booth today? There's been a big break in the Tonya Harding case. Her bodyguard was spotted this morning coming out of Dick Robertson's suite." Dick Robertson is a very popular and successful salesman with Warner TV, one of the best. I meant the joke to be a compliment to Rich.

"Actually," I went on, "Rich claims he broke his foot when he fell off his treadmill. You would too if you were carrying the weight of *Jones and Jury* and *Truth or Tabloid* around on your shoulders. To tell you the truth, I think he did it to himself deliberately so he could be the first one on the plane."

I was getting some good laughs so I went on. "We've

been having these earthquakes back in Los Angeles, so I couldn't be more thrilled to be in Miami. I'm glad to be anywhere that's not shaking. Last week I was minding my own business and out of the clear blue, Char, the psychic, called me on Friday, this is absolutely true, she's been on our show a couple of times, she called and said, 'Yo need to move the show somewhere else. This is not a good placc for you to be. Can't you pick up the phone and tell Group W you'd like to move the show?'

"I hung up and said to myself, what the hell, I'll call Derk and say, Guess what, a psychic just called me and said I have to move the show, he'll say, Fine, no problem, where would you like to go, and I'll say, I don't know . . . *King World?*"

It got a nice laugh, and I went on to say that I was just kidding and that things couldn't be better between Group W and me this year, that the show had really hit its stride, that Derk and I were getting along swell, and so on. I went on to tell them about my wonderful new hotel suite and how there on the table I found the note welcoming Rolonda Watts. That got another big laugh. I did the joke about a salesman, Tom Rose, drinking our free booze, more laughs, thanked everyone and that was it.

I returned to my table, talked to Al for a bit, then turned back to Derk just in time to hear the tail end of what he had been saying to Lou, something that included the phrase *Sturm und Drang.* Later, Al asked me what that meant, and I told him I thought it was a German phrase, meaning "storm and stress," that has come to describe what we all have to go through in life. Just then Lou slapped Derk on the shoulder and said, "At least you got beaten up by a star." God, I thought to myself.

At nine-thirty, Eduardo came over to remind Al and me that we had to catch an early flight. He suggested sneaking out. I asked him to call for the limo. At this point Derk turned, and without warning grabbed me roughly under my arm and said, "Here, let me walk you out."

While I stopped to schmooze with somebody Derk accosted Al, taking him aside and butting him in the chest with his forearms, saying, "What is the matter with your wife? Is she out of her fucking mind? You better get your wife in line!"

Al said, "I don't know what you're so upset about. All Vicki did was make a couple of jokes . . ."

"I don't think anyone knew she was joking!"

Al looked at him and as he told me later all he could think about was one of those Jerry Lewis movies where he'd get in the ring with a really big guy, and the big guy would just stand there while Jerry threw a million ineffective shots until he was creamed by one massive blow. To this day I don't know how Al managed not to knock Derk flat on his ass. Finally Al said, "If you've got a problem with Vicki, why don't you take it up with her?"

At that point, Derk came back to me, grabbed me by the arm again while shouting to Al, who had by now started to head for the exit, "Aren't you going to wait for your wife?" Al shouted back, "I'll meet you at the car, Vic." As Derk pulled me across the balcony, he whispered in my ear, "You had better start making nice-nice!"

Nice-nice?

Derk went on. "These people did not know you were joking . . ."

I tried to push him off me, which, by the way, became the basis for that ridiculous story in the *Star* (which no one has ever in the history of journalism confused with *The New York Times*) that I "punched out" Derk Zimmerman. Nothing even remotely resembling that happened. Then again, the *Star* believes that Elvis Presley is still alive, don't they?

Anyway, I said to Derk, "For chrissake, I think people know when I'm joking."

"These are salesmen! Salesmen have no sense of humor!" As he continued to hold me tight around my upper arm, I asked him if there was someone in particular who took offense? I'll talk to them. "It's too late! They're all gone! They've bailed!"

How could that be, I wondered, since Al and I were among the first to leave? As far as I could tell, everyone seemed to still be having a high old time.

Then Derk hissed one final threat under his breath. *"You are not going to be renewed,"* as he escorted me out of the hotel, like some bouncer from a two-bit dive. It was like a scene out of *The Godfather.* Full moon, Latin music, palm trees swaying. I thought to myself, "Gee, I wonder if Al Pacino knows he's missed his entrance."

As I was about to get into the limo, one of the salesmen came running up to me to ask if I'd like to say hello to Tom Rose, the fellow I had singled out for hesitating to resign, during my speech. I took that opportunity to ask if he knew that I had been kidding.

"I think so, Vicki," he said, as if amazed I even had to ask.

"Okay, just checking."

Al, who had already gotten into the limo, put his window down and asked Tom if he needed a ride anywhere. He said it would be nice if we could drop him, his wife, and two of their friends off at his hotel and we said sure. They got in, and we all had a lovely chat on the way back. When we let them out, I turned to Al and said, "I have never been so angry in my whole life."

Al said, "Wait until you hear what he did to me." For the first time, we compared our separate but similar stories.

When we arrived back at the hotel, both of us were too wound up to sleep. I suggested we go down to the bar and try to relax. We ordered doubles. It had been that kind of night.

Al went to check for messages and while he was gone, one of Group W's ad executives walked in. I asked him how he was doing.

"Fine," he said in a low, steady voice as he came over. Al returned, sat down and started talking with the fellow about golf. The bar was empty now, except for us, the piano player, the bartender, and one other couple off in the corner. Just then Derk strolled in, came over to us, put both fists squarely on the table and said to Al, "So?"

I'm thinking, So? So what? What does he want Al to do? Turn the table over and hit him?

At this point Al took my hand under the table and said, "So, it is a lovely evening and we're going out to the beach."

Derk said, "You're what?"

"It's our last night in Miami and I'm taking my wife out to the beach." He turned to me and said, "Get your drink and let's go."

Later, back in our room, we called Gregg MacGregor, our attorney, to ask if what Derk did amounted to harassment. Gregg defined it as assault. "People can't grab you," he said, "and threaten you in that manner. I'll document all this and send a letter to his attorney tomorrow."

It wasn't long after we returned to Los Angeles that we began hearing rumors from the salesmen at Group W, things like, "Houston's dumped the show." I asked Al why they would do that, we had made good friends with their station manager, whose primary goal in life had been to beat their main competition, Jerry Springer, and we'd done the job for them. I suggested Al call to find out what was really going on.

He quite graciously said he appreciated Al's calling, and explained what the problem was. He had asked Group W for three days' slack because the station was being sold. He had wanted to renew the show but needed a little extra time to close escrow. He said he then got a message on his machine from Rich Sheingold saying they'd yanked the show and given it to a competitive independent station instead. He emphasized as strongly as he could that he had *not* dumped us, that in fact he'd wanted to keep the show very badly. He said we had done great things for his station.

And that still wasn't the end. Now rumors began to fly that Group W was looking to sell the show. That was the first good news I'd heard in weeks. The more I thought about it, the more I realized that could be a dream come true.

*W*e did very well in the February 1994 ratings sweeps. Everyone connected with the show was happy. Except Derk, of course, who called to inform us that what we needed to do now was get the show "back on track."

What did that mean, I wondered. According to a private two-page memo from Derk entitled "Discussion Points for Vicki! Presentation," some of which I have excerpted here for your entertainment, there were certain goals we had yet to reach, and specific "things" that needed "fixing":

> Viewers perceive that the program is often "too loud" because Vicki sometimes shouts and screams. Along these lines, a number complain that Vicki sometimes talks too fast. A number are concerned that Vicki "swears" too much—using such words as "suck" and "bitch" too often and perhaps for shock value.

It was the same old story. Group W seemed determined to control the content of my show, and in doing so inhibit me from being the funny, loose, entertaining "personality" that Group W had hired me to be in the first place.

Almost as if some cosmic hand were guiding my fate, the best possible response to Derk's memo came the month when *Vicki!* was nominated for five Daytime Emmy Awards. Not too bad for a foul-mouthed woman

211

who talked too loud and too fast. Here, at last, I hoped, was a validation for the way I did my show. Unfortunately, we never received so much as a single phone call from Group W to congratulate us for being nominated.

Still, Group W kept reminding us of the success formula *they* had written and continued to warn us not to meddle with it. My only response was to keep reminding them that *it was Al, not Group W, who had originally conceived the show, not the other way around.*

On top of everything else came the notorious "tit-flashing" episode during the "Make Me Sexy" show that aired in February 1994. Sally Kirkland was my guest, and at one point performed a mock striptease. After which, I came out, opened my shirt and "bared my breasts"—a latex "body" I'd worn underneath with the kind of chest I only wish God had given me. And, if laughter is any indication, I'd have to say the studio audience loved it!

Nevertheless, the show was preempted in twenty-five markets and edited in God knows how many more. Hard as it is to believe, there were people who actually thought I had bared my tits on television! I told a UPI reporter who interviewed me about the incident that if it was a choice between a show about "Women with Facial Hair," which someone else had actually done the week before, frankly, I would rather look at boobs! Needless to say, all of this greatly upset Group W, in spite of the fact that even with all the preemptions and edits, the episode received an exceptionally high rating.

They sent Nancy, not me, a note about the show saying, "We have always trusted your judgment. What were you thinking?" As it happened, the joke hadn't been her idea but mine. In the midst of this latest brouhaha, Al came to me and said, "I'm really tired, Vicki. I need a change of scenery." I said I know. "So here's the deal, I'm leaving eight o'clock on Friday morning for Honolulu. I'll be on the beach by noon, and back home late Sunday night."

I said, "Oh. I thought you were coming in to ask me for a romantic weekend."

"Okay," he said, "you can come."

So we took this really decadent weekend at the Kahala Hilton. We were on the beach by noon, had a fabulous Friday night, Saturday was wonderful, Sunday we stayed on the beach all morning, then hopped a plane in the afternoon and came home. It was more fabulous because it was ridiculous!

That June, we went to New York to attend the Emmy Awards. Unfortunately we didn't win—Oprah swept, as usual—and apparently that was enough for Group W. Shortly before July, we got the news that we were canceled.

There is a natural tendency in this business to think that once a show ends, you'll never work again. Worse, when you're fired, which I'd never been until this show, you start to doubt your own talent. When I finally convinced myself I had nothing to feel guilty about, the anger set in. I wanted to hit someone. I wanted to hurt them like they had hurt me. I felt like a mother who'd had her child taken away. I wanted to put my logo on a milk carton with the following caption: "Have you seen this show?"

My daughter, Courtney, insisted for the longest time she didn't want anything to do with show business. She'd seen the roller-coaster ride close up and felt it wasn't a business at all. When she graduated from high school in 1992, she had the summer off before starting college and wanted to do something with her time. She was going to look for part-time work in Long Beach. I kept saying, "Come and be an intern on the show."

Every year, Al and I take the kids and some of their friends out on our boat to sit by the *Queen Mary* and watch the Fourth of July fireworks. We take hors d'oeu-vres, a bottle of wine, a bunch of soft drinks, and while everybody else is in traffic on the bluff, we're out there on the ocean, within spitting distance of the action.

That year, as we were bobbing around waiting for the fireworks to start, Courtney's friends were threatening to throw her overboard if she didn't take the job, because they all wanted it. Finally she gave in and said, okay, she would come and work on "the stupid show."

Her first day there she didn't know what to do or where to go, and just hoped she didn't get lost. I told her to go to the artist's entrance at NBC, right next to Jay Leno's parking spot. She asked if she should get down on her hands and knees and kiss it. I said no, that wouldn't be necessary, dear, just make a left and you'll find our show's offices.

So she came to work, and it didn't take more than two days before she got so excited meeting all the local an-chor people she sees on TV. One day she came running in and couldn't wait to tell me she'd met Branford Marsalis. A day later she breathlessly reported her first ac-tual Jay Leno sighting.

She would give me a daily rundown of who she'd seen in the hallways. Pretty soon she was rubbing elbows with such show business legends as June Allyson, Bob Conrad, Janet Leigh, Ann Blyth, Dina Merrill, Ann Miller, Mickey Rooney, Jane Russell, Virginia Mayo, Dorothy Lamour, and Dorothy Malone, all of whom had been on my show.

Before every taping I'd take questions from the audience. People always wanted to know if I still spoke to Carol Bur-nett. My standard answer was "No, I hate her, she's a bitch," which always got a big laugh. Then I would reminisce about Carol and all the fun I had doing her show. Everyone also wanted to know how I got started.

Courtney would watch these exchanges from the wings. One night when we came home from a taping and

I was in the kitchen fixing a snack, she came in and said, "Mom, the Carol Burnett show was really big, right?"

"Yes."

"Everybody knows about it, right?"

"Yes."

"So all of you are, like, a part of television history?"

"I guess we are."

She paused, looked at me wistfully, and then finally said, "I missed it, didn't I?"

That's when I thought to myself, well, she's finally seeing why Al and I fell in love with the business. Her experience on my show was the closest thing to those early wonderful, crazy days at CBS.

Mom passed away in January 1992. I'm convinced she stressed herself into illness. The closest anybody ever diagnosed what she had was Lou Gehrig's disease. My father took her to the Mayo Clinic and even they couldn't nail it down for sure. It was definitely a nerve disorder of some type that slowly deteriorated all the muscles in her body. It began in her mouth, when she discovered she could no longer taste things.

I know that people can stress themselves into illness. My dad had to have bypass surgery about eight years ago, and mom was so traumatized by the whole thing we began to worry that she might be the one who wouldn't make it through the surgery.

Dad was in Cedars-Sinai Hospital, in Beverly Hills. Joni and I went to see him the night before the operation, walked into his room, and discovered he wasn't there. But mother was.

She had every nurse on the floor attending to her. She was traumatized, she said, and was lying on dad's bed while he was down the hall getting his tests done.

Dad was cool about the whole thing. He figured he was in God's hands and that he would either live or die, while mom was an absolute wreck. She was concerned, not so much about him dying as the fact that if he left her alone she wouldn't be able to cope. To me, it was just another attempt on her part to hog all the attention, because she was jealous dad was getting a little for once. Joni fell into the trap and doted all over her, but I couldn't.

Dad got through the surgery just fine. The deal was, he had to get out of bed, walk two miles a day, and watch what he ate, and I have to say he has been religious about it. I'm really proud of him.

Mom, however, continued to worry, so much so that Joni started to think she was going to stress dad into another heart attack. I tried to reassure her that wasn't going to happen. If there's one thing I'd learned about dad, he was used to mom's antics. It was, in fact, a large part of what their relationship was about. After all, they were married almost fifty years.

Joni's a makeup artist at NBC. I saw her periodically at the studio and what can I say, she is large. She carries a lot of baggage. Literally and figuratively. One day, I was coming out of the ladies' room right by my show's offices when she walked by. She was with someone and stopped talking long enough to shoot me a dirty look. I wanted to stop her and say, "Don't you ever get tired of all of this ugliness?"

Incidentally, the only reason she has that job is because Al was able to get her into the union. She had been working part-time in the makeup department at Rexall Drugs on Hollywood Boulevard. One night she was complaining she didn't know what to do with her life, and Al asked her if she'd like to try to make a career for herself in makeup. She said yes and the next day he brought her over to CBS, where we were doing the Burnett show, and got her enough days to qualify for a union card.

How did she express her gratitude? By saying to Al on more than one occasion, "What am I supposed to do, thank you for the rest of my life?"

My feeling? Just once would be nice.

My last season, I did a *Vicki!* show called "Sexy Sisters." My guests included Jayne and Audrey Meadows. During a commercial break Jayne leaned over to me and said, "Sweetheart, how come your sister isn't here?"

I said, "Because my sister doesn't like me."

"Is she younger or older?"

"She's six years younger."

"What does she do?"

"She's in makeup right here at NBC."

"She's jealous!"

"I don't like to say that . . ."

"Of course she is!"

Maybe. I don't know. What I do know is that she got so strange when mother died as if mother had merely transcended her own body and traveled into Joni's. This in spite of the fact that they weren't particularly close.

Joni had always loved my dad more and always felt much closer to him. As far as Joni was concerned, dad was the victim, and mother was this horrible woman. Until she got ill. Then Joni became angry with me because I didn't spend enough time with mom when she was dying.

It's true, toward the end of her life, I only went to visit mom twice, maybe three times at the most. For one thing, I simply didn't have the time. I have a career and a family to raise. Joni's got a husband, who's almost never around. Jeff Hamilton (no relation to Joe) is probably among the two or three greatest jazz drummers in the world today, and spends most of his time on the road. Smart man.

Joni, by the way, was furious I didn't come to her wedding even though she'd scheduled it on a *Mama's Family* tape night. What was I supposed to do?

This was Joni's second marriage. She was married to a

Guest hosts for 'Vicki!' as impasse continues

She says, 'At this point, I am not invited back'

By Steve Brennan

Client stations of "Vicki!," the Group W talk show, expressed serious concerns Tuesday about a row between the host, Vicki Lawrence, and her producers on the cusp of the important May sweeps period. Guest hosts will be standing in for Lawrence over the next three weeks.

Lawrence, who walked off the set on Monday, was not at the studio Tuesday and said in a telephone interview, "At this point, I am not invited back."

The latest row on the show — there have been previous spats — developed over the hiring of Don Fletcher by Group W to advise on the program. Lawrence claimed that Fletcher was "spying" on her for Group W president Derk Zimmerman and she wanted Fletcher fired.

"My people were told there would be no show today, that Fletcher would be standing and that

See "VICKI!" on page 8

The Hollywood Reporter

'Vicki!'

Continued from page 3-

they would have guests in for the next three weeks," Lawrence said Tuesday.

Lawrence said she had talked to Roseanne and Tom Arnold about the situation. She also recalled that she had insisted on the firing of a producer on the show on a previous occasion.

After the producer left the show, Zimmerman had asked her to attend a Group W seminar on hiring and firing. Lawrence recalled, "I said, 'Do you think that Roseanne has been at an ABC seminar?' I said, 'You guys are trying to turn me into a corporate pinhead.'"

Concerning the latest spat, Lawrence was also critical of her executive producer, Nancy Alspaugh. "I felt she should have supported me, but she said, 'You are being irrational, you don't understand.'" When Alspaugh said they were going ahead with a production planning meeting, Lawrence replied, "Not with me . . . Do 'The Don Fletcher Show' tomorrow."

Asked if she felt that because it is a Group W-owned show the company had a right to send in a consultant, she replied, "This is the first successful show they have had in 10 years, and if something isn't broken, why fix it? And don't you discuss it with the star how you do it? . . . It's almost like we are enemies and they are taking a very hostile stance with me."

Zimmerman said in a statement, "Vicki Lawrence has informed us that her personal physician has recommended several weeks of rest. In the interim, production of 'Vicki!' will proceed with guest hosts filling in. Programs for the May sweeps have already been completed, and we are confident that the next few weeks of shows, scheduled to play over the summer, will offer viewers the high entertainment value to which they have become accustomed."

Lawrence added, "The feeling I get from Derk is that if he supports me financially and sends me flowers once in a while that I should be happy just to collect my paycheck. It's unfortunate but that's the stance he takes.

"I thought I had an agreement with Group W that if you don't have a happy star, you don't have a happy show," she continued. She also alleged, "Every time I have a problem and say to these people, 'I need your support,' they attack me legally . . . I have never been treated like this, and I am in the business 25 years."

"Vicki!" stations were worried

about the developments, coming as they do on the cusp of the May sweeps, according to Dick Kurlander, vp, director of programming at Petry Television in New York. "It's potentially very harmful to the show," said Kurlander, who added that stations are worried that the show may have repeats during the May book when "all of the competition will have very exploitable originals."

"It is distressing when the talent questions the prerogative of the company that is paying the bills," he added.

"Stations won't be terribly happy," agreed Jim Curtin, vp, director of programming at Harrington Righter & Parsons. "'Vicki!' was on a roll and showing growth," he added. The show did a 3.3 rating/14 share in the February sweeps for her second book. This represented a gain of three share points in households as well as in key female demographics. □

'Vicki!' facing sticky situation

Vicki Lawrence reportedly has become so frustrated by behind-the-scenes tensions on her Group W Prods. talkshow that she briefly threatened to air her gripes publicly on rival Tribune Entertainment talker "Geraldo."

Sources close to the situation said Lawrence bowed out of the "Geraldo" appearance yesterday in hopes the situation could be resolved without a public airing.

A spokesman for Lawrence declined to comment, but sources indicated she is under "great duress" because the situation is unresolved and her complaints have not been satisfactorily dealt with.

There have been rumblings of friction on the show since the start of the season.

Lawrence is said to have contacted Roseanne Arnold, who reportedly urged her to stand up for her rights and told her she would have gotten more response if she was a man.

— Jim Benson

Tensions resolved on 'Vicki!' set

Peace returned Friday to the set of Group W Prod.'s "Vicki!," with hostess Vicki Lawrence reportedly scoring a victory.

Sources said Group W has tentatively agreed to move senior producer Ray Giuliani to another position. Lawrence and Giuliani, a former "Geraldo" staffer, were said to be at odds, creating a great deal of tension on the show.

As previously reported (*Daily Variety*, Feb. 26), the hostess had threatened to air her gripes against Group W on the competing "Geraldo" talker at the urging of friend Roseanne Arnold, but she backed off when the production company agreed to take action.

Group W prez Derk Zimmerman said Friday that it is "too early to comment" on Giuliani's fate. Giuliani was unavailable for comment Friday.

Zimmerman, however, noted that "whatever tensions existed have been resolved."

Ironically, the behind-the-scenes turmoil came to light the same week that "Vicki!" achieved an all-time high 3.3 rating in the Nielsen national syndication ratings.

— Jim Benson

Lawrence walks off 'Vicki!' set

BY JIM BENSON

Vicki Lawrence stormed off the set of her Group W Prods.' talkshow "Vicki!" Monday morning, asserting that "interference" from the syndicator has caused her such duress that she is uncertain if she will ever return.

The disgruntled host, who had briefly threatened to take her gripes against the show public earlier this year with an appearance on the rival Tribune talker "Geraldo" (*Daily Variety*, Feb. 26, March 1), blames her departure on Group W Prods. prez Derk Zimmerman.

Turn to page 17

Lawrence cites 'interference' from syndie, walks off 'Vicki!'

Continued from page 1

Lawrence also faults exec producer and Group W vet Nancy Alspaugh, who she claims would not stand up for her, but says she has the staff's total support.

The host says the Group W topper planted a "spy" on the show, identified by Lawrence as Don Fletcher, to be his "ears and eyes" during the program's last three weeks of production this season.

Zimmerman and Lawrence discussed the acrimonious situation on Monday, with Lawrence demanding an apology. Lawrence says Zimmerman told her she was acting "totally irrational."

The Group W honcho isn't discussing many of the specific allegations raised by Lawrence, but notes the syndicator is simply seeking to improve the show — Group W's only current successful firstrun strip.

"When you get to the end of any production season, you try to fig-

ure out how to make it better for next year," he says. "We just want to build on the success that we already have."

Lawrence's role on the show remains up in the air. Before she walked out of a production planning meeting, Lawrence had been scheduled to tape six shows this week — two today, two Wednesday and two Thursday.

The only newcomer to receive a Daytime Emmy nomination this year in the host category, Lawrence has consulted with an attorney and plans to see a doctor this morning before deciding on action.

Zimmerman says the company has "nothing but the best interest of Vicki and the show at heart ... We want to do everything we can to support it."

Lawrence vehemently disagrees with that assessment.

LAWRENCE DOC SAYS GIVE IT A REST

Absent 'Vicki!' star blasts Group W president: 'Life is too short'

Vicki Lawrence, who has declared herself at war with the producer of her syndicated talkshow (*Daily Variety*, April 27), said Wednesday that her physician has ordered her to rest and avoid stress.

"Life is too short to go on working with someone like this," Lawrence said of Group W prez Derk Zimmerman. "Ours is the first hit show Group W has had in 10 years. I think he doesn't know quite how to handle it."

She said she was suffering from colitis and heart palpitations brought on by her combative relationship with Zimmerman.

As first reported here, problems escalated when Zimmerman sent consultant Donn Fletcher, a one-time senior VP of studio operations for 20th Century Fox, to the set.

Although Lawrence was told it was an attempt to improve the show and communications with her, she said she felt spied on by Fletcher, who prior to Fox served previous stints as chief executive of the discount chain the Akron and as chief operating officer of Pier 1 Imports.

Zimmerman's failure to respect Lawrence or her talent has put her "at war" with him, she said, adding that it is up to her attorney and doctor whether she'll return to the show.

Lawrence, who is under contract with Group W for next year, calls the pact a "frightening, tie-me-down kind of a deal."

Group W was forced to cancel the taping of four episodes this week after Lawrence and her husband, Al Schultz, stormed off the set Monday morning after Schultz and Fletcher reportedly had words.

Until the situation is resolved, Group W is bringing in guest hosts. Company spokesman Owen Simon confirmed that Alley Mills, who plays the mother on "The Wonder Years," is slated to tape two shows today.

One of the missed episodes was to include 50 couples from around the country who were set to wed on the show. About 10 couples didn't get word in time that the episode had been postponed and were left standing at the altar.

Shows featuring Lawrence had been taped for the May ratings sweeps, reportedly after some juggling of the schedule.

"Vicki!" ironically described as the "success story of the '90s" in trade ads, has been renewed for a second season.

From staff and Associated Press reports

Two 'Vicki!' segs canceled

Group W Prods., forced to cancel the taping of two episodes of "Vicki!" on Tuesday, is scrambling to line up guest hosts for four other episodes slated for production this week.

The syndication company took the measures after host Vicki Lawrence stormed off the set Monday, insisting that Group W was interfering in the program and not providing her with the autonomy provided to other talkshow hosts (*Daily Variety*, April 27).

A Group W spokesman said the company still holds out hope that an amicable agreement can be worked out with Lawrence, whose future with the show remains uncertain.

Warring 'Vicki!' parties in truce

By Stephen Galloway

In what must be deemed a victory for freshman talk show host Vicki Lawrence, Group W Prods. and Lawrence announced Wednesday that production on a new series of "Vicki!" installments would get under way Aug. 3, with the

See "VICKI!" on page 45

Continued from page 1—
programs to start airing nationally Sept. 13.

The announcement brought to an end — at least for now — the tempestuous battle between Lawrence (whose talk show has had the fastest rise of any such program since "The Oprah Winfrey Show") and Group W, whose president, Derk Zimmerman, had been publicly castigated by Lawrence for his interference on the show, leading to her walking off set April 26.

For now, everything was said to be coming up roses as far as the two pivotal figures were concerned. "All the problems have been resolved amicably," Zimmerman said. "We had a terrific relationship, and we have one now." When asked to define what went wrong, he said, "Show biz."

Zimmerman declined to go into the terms of the truce, but Lawrence's attorney, Gregg MacGregor, confirmed that a new contract had been drawn up, to run for another six years. That added an extra year to Lawrence's original arrangement with Group W.

More significantly, it also added extra financial incentives While neither MacGregor nor Zimmerman would go into the details, MacGregor told The Hollywood Reporter, "The best way to describe it is a recognition by both parties of the success of the program in its first year and Vicki's central role in that success."

"Vicki!" debuted Aug. 31 and has been Group W's only currently successful first-run strip, airing in 176 markets with 96% clearance in U.S. television households.

Another element in the negotiations was the role played by Lawrence's husband, makeup artist Al Schultz. Schultz, who was widely believed to be a critical factor in Lawrence's dissatisfaction (one insider described him as "the root of all the problems"), and whose closeness to her has been compared to that between Tom and Roseanne Arnold, both of whom Lawrence

consulted during her conflicts with Group W, has been given the title of consultant to Group W, with emphasis on "Vicki!"

MacGregor "completely disagreed" with the characterization of Schultz as the root of the problems. "People who've suggested that don't understand the way they work. He was very involved in an unofficial capacity in the creative life of the program. Now that's been recognized by Group W."

Concerning the two other elements of Lawrence's unhappiness — her reported dissatisfaction with executive producer Nancy Alspaugh-Jackson and her belief that one staffer, Don Fletcher, was a "spy" for Group W — MacGregor said he believed talks were ongoing for Alspaugh-Jackson to return to the show, and Zimmerman said she would continue in her present position. Both MacGregor and Zimmerman said Fletcher had already departed the program.

One final element in negotiations also seems to benefit Lawrence: Her attorney confirmed that she would be given better time slots. "The time of day the program will be aired in various markets has been updated from last year," MacGregor said, adding, "Both sides are delighted with the arrangement." □

MONDAY, MAY 3, 1993

Lawrence lashes out at Group W

By THOMAS TYRER
Staff reporter

LOS ANGELES—Vicki Lawrence said last Friday that her return to "Vicki" depends on improved relations with Group W Productions President and CEO Derk Zimmerman.

Ms. Lawrence walked off the set of "Vicki" on Monday, April 26, after Mr. Zimmerman installed Donn Fletcher as creative consultant on the program.

Group W contends the move was meant to improve the series and communications with Ms. Lawrence, but the talk show host says that Mr. Fletcher was a spy for Mr. Zimmerman.

"The way that you do a good show is to have a lot of laughter and serenity, and instead, they (Group W) seem to thrive on chaos," Ms. Lawrence told ELECTRONIC MEDIA during an emotional interview in which she compared Mr. Zimmerman's relationship with herself to an abusive husband and beaten wife.

Mr. Zimmerman would not comment beyond a statement released after Ms. Lawrence left the set last week.

"Having been informed that Vicki Lawrence's physician has recommended that she rest for several weeks, Group W Productions will continue production of the 'Vicki' series utilizing guest hosts," the statement read.

Ms. Lawrence says her stormy relationship with Mr. Zimmerman and the resulting stress has caused her health, and her pleasure in performing, to deteriorate to the point that her physician has barred her from returning to "Vicki" anytime soon.

Ms. Lawrence says the day after she left, Group W laid off her personal assistant and told the assistant to remove Ms. Lawrence's belongings from her office.

She also says Group W threatened her with a substantial lawsuit last Thursday.

"To me, the message is very clear that you're outta here, kiddo," she said.

For the week ended April 18, "Vicki" averaged a 2.6 Nielsen Television Index rating (percentage of TV households).

The show averaged a 3.4 rating and a 13 share (percentage of sets in use) during the February sweeps to rank No. 8 among all talk shows.#

News

Lawrence: I've been evicted

Group W says it's 'totally committed' to 'Vicki!'; Mills, Ferrare to host

By Steve Brennan

The ongoing saga of Vicki Lawrence's heated row with the producers and distributors of "Vicki!," the daytime talk show that she hosts, continued Friday with her claim that the company had packed up her effects at the set and sent them in boxes to her home.

Lawrence walked off the set of the show last Monday (HR 4/28). She had insisted that a consultant brought in by the show's owners, Group W, be fired. But when this did not happen she walked off and sent the producers a doctor's letter indicating she was ill.

Group W president and CEO Derk Zimmerman said in a statement, "Having been informed that Vicki Lawrence's physician has recommended that she rest for several weeks, (we) will continue production of 'Vicki!' utilizing guest hosts." He said Alley Mills of "The Wonder Years" and Christina Ferrare were signed to stand in. He stressed, "Group W Prods. remains totally committed to the series."

A Group W spokesman said on Friday that the company would not comment on Lawrence's claims that her effects had been boxed and sent from the set to her home.

Lawrence said that Zimmerman had contacted her agent to call a meeting with the host in Los Angeles.

But Lawrence insisted Friday that she would not meet Zimmer-

See **LAWRENCE** *on page 14*

Lawrence

Continued from page 3

man alone, saying, "For my own sanity and my own guts and heart, I can't see him alone."

The show's client stations have expressed concern over the row. One station rep, Dick Kurlander, vp and director of programming at Petry Television, said, "It is distressing when the talent questions the prerogative of the company that is paying the bills."

Lawrence insisted on a previous occasion that a producer be fired from the show. This led to a spat at that time also.

But this latest incident is the most publicly played drama in a reported series of on-set clashes involving Lawrence. □

TELEVISION

Lawrence takes unscheduled vacation after leaving show

NEW YORK — Vicki Lawrence, host of the daily talk show "Vicki!" is taking an unscheduled vacation from the syndicated program. It started Monday when she walked out in the midst of a production meeting.

Lawrence said she is suffering symptoms of job-related stress, and at the advice of her doctor will be off the next two weeks. The former "Carol Burnett" show star said Tuesday that the stress and her need for a breather were brought on by executives at Group W Productions, the company that produces her show.

Lawrence

According to Lawrence, Group W productions has hired someone to hang around the "Vicki" offices as a spy for Group W. That man, she said, was making her life difficult, so much it's brought on a set of physical ailments.

LAWRENCE, GROUP W RECONCILE ON 'VICKI!'

BY JIM BENSON

In a move that had been expected (*Daily Variety,* June 14), Group W Prods. and entertainer Vicki Lawrence have resolved their differences and agreed to go ahead with a second season of the syndicated talkshow "Vicki!"

Group W has given into a number of the hostess' demands, including the primary condition that she be given more creative control over the program.

Under the new pact, Lawrence will gain the added title of co-exec producer with Group W vet Nancy Alspaugh, who helmed the show during its first season.

Additionally, Lawrence's husband, Al Schultz, will be given the title of Group W creative consultant.

Lawrence's attorney, Greg McGregor, said Schultz had been serving in a similar role during the first season without pay and the title is in recognition of his contributions.

The new contract, which McGregor said also includes an "adjustment" in Lawrence's financial package, is bound to disappoint some competing syndicators itching to upgrade their own talkshows into "Vicki!" time slots.

"Vicki!" is currently cleared in 174 markets covering 96% of the country. Group W had renewed the show in a large chunk of the U.S. before the internal spat spilled into the public spotlight just prior to the May sweeps.

Group W prez Derk Zimmer-man said that while a handful of stations held off on renewals until the situation was resolved, none of them committed to a spate of other chat shows.

The reconciliation brings to an end the publicity war that Lawrence has waged against Zimmerman since she left the show in a huff, insisting that she needed more creative control and demanding more respect from the Group W topper.

On Wednesday, however, Lawrence sounded more like Rodney King than Rodney Dangerfield, urging everyone to get along.

"I think what Derk and I have both learned is that we need to sit down once in a while and chat," she said in a statement. "...Derk Zimmerman and I have re-established the fact that we believe in each other as much as we did when we launched this sucker."

Zimmerman said that Lawrence "won't have to do things she doesn't want to do" from now on. He also noted the addition of Schultz as a Group W consultant "will be real positive for us and the show."

Production will resume Aug. 3, with the second season of shows slated to begin airing Sept. 13.

Despite the negative publicity surrounding Lawrence's absence during the May sweeps, partial Nielsen sweeps results indicate the show managed to boost the time period average share by 25% over the previous May — with some station reps speculating that more viewers watched out of curiosity.

drummer the first time as well. I understand that musician thing. Musicians are attractive people. Elizabeth Ashley has a wonderful theory about men. I once heard her talk about it I think on the Dinah Shore show many years ago. When a man is doing what a man does best, whether it's pounding nails, or drumming drums, or brain surgery, he is very attractive. Liz said, the test of true love is, do you still love that man when he's puking in the toilet.

However, the real reason I didn't visit mom more often is, quite frankly, because I just didn't love her anymore. As far back as I can remember, she was never satisfied with anything I did, or anyone I chose to be with. She never had anything nice to say about my home or my husband. It was almost like Al didn't exist to her, like our marriage didn't exist. The single worst thing she did, and what proved the breaking point, happened when Courtney was eight.

She and Garrett went to grandma and grandpa's house for the weekend. This was a big deal for them, because it was only the second weekend my parents ever took the kids. The first, you'll remember, mom brought them home the same day three hours later because she couldn't deal with it.

Anyway, the kids went to their grandparents for the weekend, and when they came home, Courtney was behaving very strangely. I went to kiss her good night and she pulled away from me. I kept on asking her what was wrong and all she would say was that she didn't want to talk about it. This went on for three nights, not very typical of our family. We're very touchy, feely, huggy folks and talk about everything. I sat down on her bed one night and said I wasn't leaving the room until she told me what was going on. She said she had promised she wouldn't tell. I said, "Who do you promise you won't talk to your mother?"

After much gentle prodding, she broke down and confessed.

During her visit, mom had sat down with the scrapbooks and the photo albums she'd kept and proceeded to tell Courtney all about Bobby, that he was a songwriter, and asked if she knew of him. In our family we talk about everything, so Courtney said yes, and knew that we had been divorced. Then mother asked Courtney if she knew her birthdate, and Courtney said yes. "Well," mom said, "have you ever calculated from the time your parents were married until the time you were born? Because it's not nine months."

Thank God, Courtney knew that too, because she had seen a pillow someone once gave us, with our wedding anniversary in needlepoint. She came in one night when Al and I were cooking dinner and said, "I was just in your room counting, and this doesn't come to nine months." I went, Oh God! I'd known this was going to happen! I got hysterical, while Al calmly took her in the other room, sat her down and explained how mommy and daddy had been in love, and were so excited they couldn't wait to have her.

During that weekend, mom told Courtney that Al hadn't been in love with me and that the only reason we got married was because we had to. I sat there and talked to Courtney for the longest time. She cried her heart out, I cried my heart out, we held each other, and I knew then that she felt better for talking to me about it. After all, that was a lot for a little kid to hold in.

I called my mom the next day and said, "How dare you?"

She totally denied all of it and insisted Courtney was lying. At that point I asked Al what kind of a mother does this? Why would she hate us so much she would turn our kids against us? That was the breaking point that destroyed my love for her. Up until then no matter what she pulled I could still say you're my mother, I love you, even if I don't like you all that much. But after what she pulled with Courtney, that was the last straw.

So no, I didn't run down to Palm Springs every minute and visit her. Not even when dad decided to move mom into a convalescent home. There are a lot of nice places that really cater to older people in Palm Springs, but dad found it too depressing. It didn't take him long to decide he'd rather have her home. So he ended up moving into a very nice house and hiring a full-time nurse to watch after mom.

Shortly thereafter, dad wanted to have everyone down for Thanksgiving. The family made the trip and mom was a little too thrilled to see me, which I think bothered Joni even more than my not coming would have.

I could see that mom was really ill and that she wasn't going to last much longer. I remember sitting by her bedside and wanting to say to her, "I'm sorry," but I felt like I'd spent so much of my life doing just that, I couldn't say it anymore.

For a long time, I had suspected mom was addicted to drugs. I confirmed this when she asked me that day, "Would you go in the bathroom and get me a painkiller?"

I asked her where they were and she told me in the top middle drawer in the bathroom. It was about a foot wide and a foot deep. I opened it and I swear it must have been stuffed to the rim with medications! Later, as she was drifting off she said, "Your dad doesn't like me to say it, but I've been saving up enough sleeping pills to kill myself."

Man, I thought, some things never change. If you really wanted to, all you'd have to do was get yourself a bottle of Evian and empty that bathroom drawer.

When she finally did pass away, I told Al, like that song says in *A Chorus Line, I felt nothing!*

It was Joni who called with the news that mother had died, adding that dad didn't want me to come down. I asked why and she was very abrupt, saying only, "Dad doesn't really want you there."

I hung up and called him. He said, "There's no need to come down. We're really not going to do anything. Your mother wanted to be cremated, so that's what I'm going to do." It was almost as if he wanted to sweep the whole thing under the carpet.

"Aren't you going to have a memorial service?" I asked.

"No. We're just going to go ahead and cremate."

That night, I dreamt about my mother. At one point, I woke up and Al held me while I cried. I asked him to explain how somebody can die without even a memorial service, or some type of ceremonial goodbye. Don't you have to have a period at the end of a sentence?

I called dad the next morning and said I was coming down, that I felt I needed to be there with him. "Fine," he said. Joni, Miss Happyface, was there, and at first wouldn't speak to me. Courtney came along to console dad, but as it turned out he didn't seem to need it. He was doing quite well. By the time I arrived the body had already been cremated. So I never really had an opportunity to say goodbye after all. At some point during my visit Joni started screaming and yelling at me about all that I hadn't done for mom. Even Courtney said, "You three are all you have left. Whatever is the past, is the past." Dad agreed, adding it was all under the bridge now and asked Joni if we couldn't bury the hatchet and get along with each other. Joni said no, she couldn't. She then asked if I would step outside with her for a minute. I did and she started screaming at me. *You actresses are all alike. All selfish bitches!"*

It was like a scene out of *Mama's Family*. All I could think of was, boy, I bet the neighbors are just loving this!

It was, all in all, a disappointing day, at the end of which I said goodbye to dad and decided to drive back home. He called a couple of days later and that's when I realized for the first time how little we ever really talked while mom was alive. It wasn't until she died that I actually spoke to him, and have since come to realize that I probably got my sense of humor from him. He has a very sharp, nicely understated wit. "Victoria?" He likes to call me Victoria when he wants to make a point. "I have your mother here." (He meant her ashes.) "I'm taking her to Hawaii tomorrow to bury her."

I said, "Oh, good."

"You know how much your mother loved to shop? She would be thrilled to know she was going to Hawaii in an I. Magnin bag."

"I . . . I guess so, dad . . ."

It turns out that I enjoy my mother more now for the simple reason that I can finally get a word in edgewise when I talk to her up at Punchbowl, the military cemetery on Oahu, *and the amazing thing is she listens without interrupting!*

I thought perhaps after a little time went by, my relationship with Joni might improve. After all, mom had spent a lifetime playing us against each other. The net effect of her method (or her madness, who knows) was to keep Joni and me apart. Mom would call Joni and say, "Vicki said this," and then she'd call me and say, "Joni said that," then Joni and I wouldn't speak to each other. I remember finally going to my sister one time and saying, "If you want to hear what really happened, call me, because I don't think we're getting the same story from mom." Unfortunately, the emotional distance between us remains high, wide, and deep.

Trudy Otterson, the gal who did all my wardrobe on *Mama's Family,* dressed me every week for five years. When somebody sees you buck naked week in and week out they get to know you fairly well, and you them. One year for my birthday, Trudy sent me a pillow she top-stitched that said, "If Mom's not happy, nobody's happy." I put it up in my kitchen and it's still there to this day. The kids laugh about it, but it's true. You have to be happy.

When I think about my mom, I can see she wasn't happy with her life. The tragedy is, she had every opportunity to change it and didn't.

I know that when we were living in Hawaii, I was miserable, and therefore so were the kids. When I returned to the mainland and began *Mama's Family,* they'd stand in the driveway every morning and go, "Have a great day! Have fun at work, mom!" *They knew.*

My dad called one day in December 1993, and during our conversation I asked him if he wanted to come over Christmas Eve. He said he was going to spend that night with Joni. "Okay, then," I said, "come over Christmas Day." He wanted to know if it was all right if he spent the night, as he was going to be with his new girlfriend. I said, "Sure dad," and told him he could stay in what we call the "Lucy/Desi" guest room because it has twin beds.

Anyway, dad said okay, and then called again a few days later to ask if he could stay with us on Christmas Eve as well. He said that my sister wouldn't let him sleep with another woman in her home, because it would destroy her memory of mom. My reaction was, hey, dad's seventy-six years old, if he wants to sleep with a woman, that's his business. "Well," I told him, "you're welcome to bring the tramp and sleep with her here, dad."

I couldn't believe Joni's lack of sensitivity. Who did she think she was, *not approving of his lifestyle!* I mean, come on! When I was growing up, no matter what you were arguing about with dad, my favorite thing he used to say, especially when you were about to make your point, was, "Well, that's what makes horse races."

*V*icki! has proved an incredible springboard for me, one hell of a two-year ride. Among other things, it let people know that I am *me,* not Mama, and in doing so has torn down a lot of walls that would have otherwise still been in my way.

Still, in the scheme of things, my career is last on my list of life's priorities. The first is my family, and what I've learned from them.

From Al, I got my independence. He was the first person who ever made me feel sexy, and good about myself. Al has been so incredibly supportive there's no way I would be where I am today without him. It seems I've always had people trying to change me. No one ever let me be me and accepted me for who and what I am, except Al.

When the babies were really young, I bought every child-rearing book in the world. My favorite was *Help! I'm a Parent*. I'd have them all out, prepared for anything, and when something didn't quite work the way I'd wanted it to, Al would remind me that the important thing to remember about kids was that they were given to us by God for eighteen years to kind of lead and help and guide. As they mature, they develop their own ideas and feelings, and you're not always going to agree with them. So, if you raise them to be independent, when they assert themselves as individuals you can't get pissed at them.

My daughter, Courtney, is the most special lady. She's so smart about so many things. She is my very best girl-friend, we laugh like crazy, and there is absolutely nothing about which I cannot talk to her. She has made me more aware of the world around me, where I fit into it, and the consequences of my own actions. She's very thoughtful and empathetic. She gets into other people's souls.

As for Garrett Lawrence Schultz, well, what can I say, I really love this guy to death! I guess the most amazing thing about him is something that both Al and I could take a lesson from: the way he always asks if anything is really worth getting all bent out of shape over. Here is a kid who stresses over nothing. One day a couple of weeks ago I got so upset over the VCR because Al had asked me to tape a T.V. show while he was out sailing. I tried, but wasn't able to get the machine to work. I couldn't figure out the instructions, went through them twenty times, and got so frustrated I wound up on the bedroom floor crying! That's when Garrett came in and said, "What's the matter?"

I tried to explain through my tears and he said, "Mom, it's a VCR. Pull it together." He watches as we go through the hard times and loves nothing better than to see us happy. So, from Garrett we've tried to learn to lay back and keep things in perspective. You're supposed to be having fun, he keeps telling us. His first priority is to have a great time in life, and maybe that's not so bad.

I've learned so many things from Carol Burnett. Like sharing and giving. More than once she has said to me, "Vicki, anybody can open a door for you, but you're the one who has to walk through. You don't owe me anything, really." I still disagree with that, and believe I owe everything to her, but she won't hear of it. "No," she insists, "you don't owe anybody anything. When you say thank you and move on, you're the one who has to run with the ball." On a day-to-day basis, down in the trenches, I don't believe there has ever been anybody in this business more generous or giving than Carol. She's a very special lady.

When I first got embroiled with Group W, Carol's advice was to be a good little girl. However, when things escalated, we had dinner one night and she said, "My God, I don't understand how old you have to be or how long your résumé before someone will hand you the baton."

Perhaps the most important lesson of my life is that you have to believe in yourself, to know what you're worth, know when to fight for it, and know when to move on.

Hawaii has always been a special place for Al and me.

One day, not too long after my show was canceled, Al said, "I'm taking you to Honolulu. You deserve it."

I slept the entire way over on the plane. The first thing we did when we arrived was to take a walk on the beach. I noticed a book someone was reading: *Your Body Believes Every Word You Say.* Boy, that's the truth, I thought. I breathed the balmy air that went all the way down to my toes and decided it was time to be happy again.

Everywhere we went people stopped to tell me how much they loved the show. At first I would say thanks, but I was canceled you know, until it dawned on me that when someone tells you how much they love you, you don't have to explain anything. It isn't necessary. So I stopped trying and accepted their good wishes.

It was a wonderful vacation. We rested a lot, swam a lot, read a lot, smiled a lot. I noticed that my stomach was beginning to function normally again. I came home with a new attitude. I started reading all the stacks of mail that had piled up since June. I began thinking less of myself and more about all the people whose lives I had the good fortune to touch on a daily basis—the half of my television relationship that doesn't get seen—my fans.

Epilogue

It has been most enjoyable to collaborate on this book with Marc Eliot. There's something to be learned from every person with whom you come into contact in your life, and Marc is no exception. On his final visit to a *Vicki!* taping, he had a brief backstage conversation with Nancy Alspaugh. She was surprised to see him and said, "What are you doing here?"

"I thought I'd catch the taping," he said. Actually, he was there to check out my guests, who that day happened to all be gorgeous supermodels.

"How's that book coming?" Nancy inquired.

"Pretty much done," Marc said.

"I would have thought you'd need to write a new ending."

"Nancy," Marc replied, "in life there are no endings."

He walked away and she stared at him, a bit puzzled.

I laughed at the story when I heard it. However, over the past few months I've thought often about it. As my life races through middle age at warp speed, with more twists and turns than Space Mountain, I've been reminded of Marc's words over and over again: "There are no endings."

Some time ago I read an article by a psychologist who said that if the average person knew what was going to happen to them in the next five years they would probably commit suicide. So I guess the answer is, take one day at a time. As I always say, life is much too serious to be taken seriously. So, for God's sake, kids, keep laughing. Each day is a new adventure. And remember, there are no endings . . .

Only new beginnings.

To be continued . . .

Index

Page numbers in *italics* refer to illustrations.